BBC

ITALIAN
GRAMMAR

KT-142-079

Author
Alwena Lamping

Consultant
Denise De Rôme

Developed by the BBC Language Unit
Edited by Jenny Cripps
Project managed by Stenton Associates
Proofread by Paola Boutall
Produced by **AMR**
Original design by Oxprint Design
Cover artwork by Elaine Cox

© Alwena Lamping 1995

ISBN 0 563 39943 0

Published by BBC Books, a division of BBC Worldwide Ltd
Woodlands, 80 Wood Lane, London W12 0TT
First published 1995

Text and cover printed by Clays Ltd, St Ives Plc

Also available:
    BBC French Grammar
    BBC German Grammar
    BBC Spanish Grammar

Introduction

The BBC Italian Grammar is aimed at adult learners, whether learning at home or on Adult/Further Education or non-specialist Higher Education language courses. It is also ideal for GCSE students.

It is a practical reference book which sets out to make Italian grammar accessible to English-speaking learners, and it is the perfect complement to any course book. The emphasis is on clear and concise explanation of the core structures of Italian, illustrated by examples using current, everyday language.

It is not necessary to have detailed formal knowledge of English grammar to use this book, since the use of technical grammatical terms has been restricted to those which are essential. There is also a glossary to help clarify these terms.

The book is designed to allow easy and rapid consultation. It comprises:

- a list of contents – a quick way to find the section or sub-section you want;

- a glossary of grammatical terms;

- grammar explanations clearly laid out in numbered sections and subsections. The first half of the book covers nouns, articles, adjectives, adverbs, pronouns and prepositions. The second half focuses on verbs: their formation, use and irregular forms.

- verb tables – the patterns for regular verbs and for commonly used irregular verbs;

- a comprehensive, easy-to-use index, which lists key words in Italian and English as well as grammatical terms.

Contents

Contents

adjective

Adjectives are words which describe or give information about nouns or pronouns. There are several categories:

*a **new** hotel, the rooms are **large**, it is **white*** (descriptive)
***our** hotel, **their** rooms* (possessive)
***this** hotel, **those** rooms* (demonstrative)
***any** hotel, **every** room* (indefinite)
***which** hotel?, **how many** rooms?* (interrogative)

adverb

Adverbs are words which add information to verbs, adjectives or other adverbs.

*We walked **quickly** and I am **rather** tired.*
*She speaks **very clearly**.*

agreement

In Italian, the form of adjectives, articles, pronouns and past participles is dependent on whether the noun or pronoun they accompany is masculine or feminine, singular or plural; this is called agreement.

article

There are two types of article in English: definite (*the*), indefinite (*a/an*). Italian also has the partitive, which is equivalent to 'some' or 'any'. They are all used before nouns.

auxiliary verbs

Auxiliary verbs are used together with other verbs, particularly when forming compound tenses.

*she **has** been here, we **have** eaten, I **did**n't go*
In Italian, the auxiliary verbs are **avere** and **essere**.

comparative

Comparative forms of adjectives and adverbs are used to make comparisons.

*This seat is **more comfortable** than that one. It's **softer**.*
*I don't go to France **as often as** I go to Italy.*
*I go **less frequently**.*

conditional

The conditional expresses what WOULD happen, usually involving certain conditions.

*I **would play** if I hadn't hurt my knee.*

*He **would have gone** but he was very busy.*

feminine (see gender)

gender

The gender of a noun indicates whether it is masculine or feminine. In Italian every noun is either masculine or feminine.

gerund

A gerund is the form of the verb which in English ends in *-ing* and is used as a noun.

***Travelling** in Italy is wonderful.*

It is used differently in Italian.

imperative

The imperative mood is used to give instructions or commands and to make suggestions.

***Put** it on the table.*

***Shut** the door!*

***Let's go** to the cinema.*

infinitive

The infinitive is the form of a verb which does not show any person or tense. It is the form found in a dictionary.

(to) arrive, (to) buy,(to) have, (to) like

interrogative

Interrogative words are used to ask questions.

***Which** watch did you buy? (adjective)*

***Which one** do you prefer? (pronoun)*

***Where** did you buy it? (adverb)*

invariable

An invariable word does not change its form to agree with another word.

irregular

A noun or verb is said to be irregular when it does not follow the pattern for a similar group of nouns or verbs.

masculine (see gender)

modal verb

A modal verb is followed by another verb. In English, modal verbs include *can, could, may, might, must, ought*.

*You **must** hurry. We **ought** to leave now.*
*I **could** help you.*

The main modal verbs in Italian are **dovere**, **potere** and **volere**.

negative

Negative words indicate that something is NOT done.

*I am **not** going. She **never** writes to us.*
***Nobody** spoke. They said **nothing**.*

noun

A noun is a word which names a person, a thing, a place, or an abstract idea such as an emotion or a quality.

Paul, visitors, book, rain, Italy, airport, love, difficulty

number

Number differentiates between singular (one) and plural (more than one).

***This** new **book** is interesting. (singular)*
***These** new **books** are interesting. (plural)*

object

The object of a verb is a noun or a pronoun which is affected by the action of a verb.

*I bought **some cards** and posted **them**. (direct object)*
*I sent a card **to Daniel**. I sent **him** a card. (indirect object)*

passive

The passive voice is used when something is done TO the subject, rather than BY the subject.

The tour was led by an Italian guide. (passive)
An Italian guide led the tour. (active)

past participle

The past participle of a verb is the form used after 'has', 'have' or 'had', when referring to past actions, and in passive constructions.

*I have **finished**, she has **won**, the bill had been **paid**.*

person

Person is a way of classifying verb forms and pronouns.
First person refers to the speaker or to a group which includes the speaker.
Second person refers to the person addressed.
Third person refers to a third party – anyone or anything else.

plural (see number)

possessive

A possessive is a word which shows ownership or possession.

my, your, his, her, its, our, your, their (possessive adjectives)
mine, yours, his, hers, ours, yours, theirs (possessive pronouns)

preposition

Prepositions are words such as *at, to, from, with, until*, which are used before a noun or a pronoun. They often refer to time or place.

*I'll meet you **at** one o'clock **at** the station.*
*Put it **in** the cupboard **until** tomorrow.*

pronoun

A pronoun is a word which is used instead of a noun, sometimes to avoid repeating that noun.

*Anna lent **me** a map and **I** gave **it** back to **her**.*
*My pen is broken; can **I** use **yours**?*

There are several categories of pronouns: personal pronouns, which include subject and object pronouns, and demonstrative, indefinite, interrogative, possessive, reciprocal, reflexive and relative pronouns.

regular

Regular nouns and verbs follow a predictable pattern.

singular (see number)

subject

The subject of a verb indicates who or what is carrying out the action of the verb.

My friend arrives today. *She's* coming from Rome.

subjunctive

The subjunctive mood is used when expressing opinions, wishes, possibilities and doubt. It is used more widely in Italian than in English.

If I *were* you, I'd go. It is essential that you *be* there.

superlative

Superlative forms express the highest degree of adjectives and adverbs.

This is the *most comfortable* seat. It's the *softest*.

I've bought the *least expensive* ticket.

George drives *the most quickly/the fastest*.

tense

Tense indicates when the action of the verb takes place – past, present or future.

I *worked*, I *was working*, I *work*, I *will work*

verb

A verb is a word which refers to an action or state. The form of a verb changes to show person and tense.

I *like*, you *have*, she *eats*, we *ate*, they *have eaten*

2.1 The Italian alphabet

The Italian alphabet has 21 letters.

a	a	h	acca	q	qu
b	bi	i	i	r	erre
c	ci	l	elle	s	esse
d	di	m	emme	t	ti
e	e	n	enne	u	u
f	effe	o	o	v	vu
g	gi	p	pi	z	zeta

j (i lunga), k (cappa), w (doppia vu), x (ics) and y (ipsilon) are used to spell out foreign words.

2.2 Pronunciation

The sounds of Italian are consistent – they do not vary from one word to another. Similar sounds occurring in English words are indicated below.

■ 2.2.1 Vowels

Italian vowel sounds are pure and always pronounced distinctly, even when there are two or more next to each other. a, i and u have one sound each, e and o have two possible sounds – open or closed, so called because of the open or near-closed position of the jaw when pronouncing them.

a		barba	father
e	open	penna	pen
	closed	perché/sera	case
i		isola	meet
o	open	pollo	polish
	closed	voce	pour
u		musica	cool

■ 2.2.2 Consonants

Most consonants sound very similar in Italian and English. However, the following letters and combinations of letters need special attention.

c		
ce/ci	**cena/arrivederci**	**chess/chip**
c + other letters	**caro/classe**	**car/class**
	chilo	**kilo**

g		
ge/gi	**gelato/magico**	**jet/magic**
gn	**lasagne/signora**	**canyon**
gli	**bottiglia/gli**	**million**
g + other letters	**grande/spaghetti**	**get/rag**

h		
	ho/hotel	**honour** (not sounded)

r		
	raro	strong sound as in the Scottish pronunciation of English

s		
s	**salute**	**sat**
s between two vowels	**riposo**	**rose**
sce/sci	**pesce/sci**	**shepherd/ship**
sc + other letters	**scuola/schermo**	**school/skip**

z		
	zanzara	**pads**
	zio	**pits**

Double consonants have the same sound as single consonants but they are pronounced more emphatically and the sound is prolonged.

nn	**panna**	**unnatural**

2.3 Stress

As a general rule, Italian words have the stress on the last syllable but one:

madre *mother,* al**ber**go *hotel,* carto**li**na *postcard*

... unless there is a written accent indicating a stressed final vowel:

difficol**tà** *difficulty,* caf**fè** *coffee,* arrive**rò** *I will arrive*

There are many exceptions to the general rule. Most of the exceptions have the stress on the third syllable from the end:

sabato *Saturday,* te**le**fono *telephone,* eco**no**mico *cheap*

A few have the stress on the fourth syllable from the end:

abitano *they live,* man**da**temelo *send it to me*

2.4 Accents

Accents are used in Italian:

- to indicate a stressed final vowel:
  cit**tà** *town,* caf**fè** *coffee,* co**sì** *so,* pe**rò** *however,* più *more*

- to distinguish between two words that look and sound identical:

dà *gives*	sì *yes*	è *is*
da *from*	si *himself/herself*	e *and*

■ **2.4.1** Two accents are used – acute ['] and grave [`].

- The acute accent is used on a closed e:
  perché *because,* né ... né *neither ... nor*
  It can also be used on a closed o, but this is very rare

- The grave accent is used on the open e and o:
  è *is,* cioè *that is,* ciò *that,* però *however*
  It is also used on vowels which do not have both open and closed sounds: verità *truth,* così *so,* più *more*

An alternative convention exists for **i** and **u**, which can be marked as closed vowels with an acute accent: **cosí**, **piú**. However, the use of the grave accent on all vowels except the closed **e** and (rarely) **o** is considered good standard Italian and is prevalent in most dictionaries, books and newspapers.

2.5 Capital letters

Italian uses capital letters much less frequently than English.

■ **2.5.1** Capital letters are used:
- at the beginning of a sentence.

- for names of people, places and institutions:
  Giovanna abita a Siena. *Giovanna lives in Siena.*
  l'Unione Europea *the European Union*, l'ONU *the UN*

- for some dates and festivals:
  il Trecento *the 14th century*, Natale *Christmas*

- sometimes for **Lei**, **Loro** and **Voi** (*you*), and related pronouns and adjectives like **La**, **Le**, **Suo**, **Vi**, **Vostro**. This applies particularly in commercial correspondence:
  La ringraziamo per la Sua lettera. *Thank you for your letter.*

■ **2.5.2** Capital letters are NOT used for:
- **io** (*I*), except at the beginning of a sentence.

- titles followed by a surname:
  la signora Perrone *Mrs Perrone*, il dottor Valletta *Dr Valletta*

- names of days or months:
  giovedì *Thursday*, marzo *March*

- languages, peoples or adjectives of nationality:
  Parlo inglese. *I speak English.*
  gli italiani *the Italians*, i gallesi *the Welsh*
  un paese europeo *a European country*

3 Nouns

A noun is a word which denotes people, animals, objects, places and abstract concepts – **sorella** *(sister)*, **gatto** *(cat)*, **macchina** *(car)*, **Sicilia** *(Sicily)*, **ristorante** *(restaurant)*, **libertà** *(freedom)*.

Most Italian nouns are regular, ending in -o, -a or -e in the singular. These endings change in the plural.

Some nouns are irregular and need to be learnt separately.

3.1 Gender

In Italian every noun is either masculine or feminine, regardless of whether it is a living being, an inanimate object or an abstract quality. It is important to know the gender of a noun in order to select the correct form of adjectives and articles which have masculine and feminine forms.

3.2 Regular nouns ending in -o

Nouns ending in -o are nearly all masculine:

un biglietto	*a ticket*
il supermercato	*the supermarket*
mio fratello	*my brother*

■ **3.2.1** To form the plural, -o changes to -i:

due biglietti	*two tickets*
i supermercati	*the supermarkets*
i miei fratelli	*my brothers*

■ **3.2.2** Spelling notes

- Nouns ending in -io drop one i in the plural:

il figlio *son*	i figli *sons*
il bacio *kiss*	i baci *kisses*

... unless the i is stressed:

lo zio *uncle*	gli zii *uncles*

- Most nouns ending in -**co** or -**go** add **h** in the plural to retain the hard sound of the **c** and **g**:

il par**co** *park*	i par**chi** *parks*
il la**go** *lake*	i la**ghi** *lakes*

  Some do not add **h** and the plural therefore has a soft **c** or **g** sound. Most of these have a vowel before -**co** and -**go**:

l'ami**co** *friend*	gli ami**ci** *friends*
l'aspara**go** *asparagus*	gli aspara**gi** *asparagus*

3.3 Regular nouns ending in -a

Nouns ending in -**a** are usually feminine:

una birra	*a beer*
la macchina	*the car*
mia figlia	*my daughter*

■ **3.3.1** To form the plural, -**a** changes to -**e**:

due birre	*two beers*
le macchine	*the cars*
le mie figlie	*my daughters*

■ **3.3.2** Spelling notes

- Nouns ending in -**ca** or -**ga** add **h** in the plural to retain the hard sound of the **c** and **g**:

la bar**ca** *boat*	le bar**che** *boats*
la casalin**ga** *housewife*	le casalin**ghe** *housewives*

- Nouns ending in -**cia** or -**gia** usually drop the **i**:

la spiag**gia** *beach*	le spiag**ge** *beaches*
l'aran**cia** *orange*	le aran**ce** *oranges*

  ... unless the **i** is stressed or -**cia**/-**gia** follows a vowel:

la farma**cia** *chemist's shop*	le farma**cie** *chemist's shops*
la vali**gia** *suitcase*	le vali**gie** *suitcases*

3.4 Regular nouns ending in -e

Some nouns ending in **-e** are masculine, while others are feminine.

masculine	feminine
il cane *dog*	la carne *meat*
il nome *name*	la notte *night*
il valore *value*	la valle *valley*

■ **3.4.1** To form the plural of both the masculine and feminine, **-e** changes to **-i**.

masculine	feminine
i cani *dogs*	le carni *meats*
i nomi *names*	le notti *nights*
i valori *values*	le valli *valleys*

■ **3.4.2** A few nouns ending in **-e** exist in both masculine and feminine forms with quite different meanings.

masculine	feminine
il capitale *money*	la capitale *capital city*
il fine *aim*	la fine *end*
il fronte *front*	la fronte *forehead*

■ **3.4.3** On the whole, it is not possible to tell whether nouns ending in **-e** are masculine or feminine, but some of them can be grouped.

- Most nouns ending in **-ore** or **-ale** are masculine:
  il trattore *tractor*, il motore *engine*
  l'animale *animal*, il giornale *newspaper*

- Most nouns ending in **-ice** or **-udine** are feminine:
  l'attrice *actress*, l'imperatrice *empress*
  l'abitudine *habit*, l'attitudine *aptitude*

- Most nouns ending in **-ione** are feminine:
  la stazione *station*, la televisione *television*

Regular nouns

	singular	plural
masculine	-o	-i
feminine	-a	-e
masculine and feminine	-e	-i

3.5 Irregular nouns

Irregular nouns are nouns which do not follow the patterns shown above.

■ **3.5.1** A few nouns ending in **-o** are feminine. They are invariable, i.e. they do not change in the plural:

la radio *radio*	le radio *radios*
la foto *photograph*	le foto *photographs*
la moto *motorbike*	le moto *motorbikes*

... except

| la mano *hand* | le mani *hands* |

■ **3.5.2** Most nouns ending in **-ma** are masculine. The plural ends in **-mi**:

il problema *problem*	i problemi *problems*
il programma *programme*	i programmi *programmes*
l'aroma *aroma*	gli aromi *aromas*

... except

il cinema *cinema*	i cinema *cinemas*
il clima *climate*	i clima *climates*
la vittima *victim*	le vittime *victims*

■ **3.5.3** The following nouns do not change in the plural.

- Nouns ending in -**à**, which are all feminine:
  la città *town, city*   le città *towns*
  la difficoltà *difficulty*   le difficoltà *difficulties*

- Nouns ending in other accented vowels:
  il caffè *coffee/bar*   i caffè *bars*
  il tassì *taxi*   i tassì *taxis*
  la virtù *virtue*   le virtù *virtues*

- Nouns ending in -**i** or -**ie**:
  il brindisi *toast (drink)*   i brindisi *toasts*
  la crisi *crisis*   le crisi *crises*
  la specie *species*   le specie *species*

... except
  la moglie *wife*   le mogli *wives*

- Words borrowed from other languages:
  il computer   i computer
  lo chef   gli chef
  la hostess *air hostess*   le hostess

■ **3.5.4** Some nouns are masculine in the singular and feminine in the plural:

l'uovo *egg*	le uova *eggs*
il lenzuolo *sheet*	le lenzuola *sheets*
il paio *pair*	le paia *pairs*
il braccio *arm*	le braccia *arms*
il dito *finger*	le dita *fingers*
un centinaio *about a hundred*	centinaia *hundreds*

■ **3.5.5** A few nouns have very irregular plural forms:
  l'uomo *man*   gli uomini *men*
  il dio *god*   gli dei *gods*

3.6 Nouns referring to people

Some nouns referring to people have separate masculine and feminine forms, others have one form for both.

■ **3.6.1** Many nouns have a masculine form ending in -o or -e and a feminine form ending in -a:

il cugino *cousin*	la cugina *cousin*
il nonno *grandfather*	la nonna *grandmother*
il signore *gentleman*	la signora *lady*
il padrone *owner*	la padrona *owner*

■ **3.6.2** Some nouns have a feminine form ending in -essa:

il professore *teacher*	la professoressa *teacher*
lo studente *student*	la studentessa *student*
l'avvocato *lawyer*	l'avvocatessa *lawyer* (see 3.6.8)

■ **3.6.3** Some nouns ending in -tore have a feminine equivalent ending in -trice (but see also 3.6.8):

il direttore *manager*	la direttrice *manageress*
l'attore *actor*	l'attrice *actress*

... except

il dottore *doctor*	la dottoressa *doctor*

■ **3.6.4** There are many nouns referring to males or females ending in -e:

il contabile *accountant*	la contabile *accountant*
l'insegnante *teacher*	l'insegnante *teacher*
il nipote *nephew, grandson*	la nipote *niece, granddaughter*

Articles and adjectives used with these nouns must be masculine or feminine as appropriate:

Mario è il nuovo insegnante.	*Mario is the new teacher.*
Anna è una brava insegnante.	*Anna is a good teacher.*

■ **3.6.5** Nouns ending in **-ista** have the same form in the singular for men and women, but separate plural forms:

singular	plural
il/la turista *tourist*	i turisti/le turiste *tourists*
il/la giornalista *journalist*	i giornalisti/le giornaliste *journalists*

Similarly:

il/la collega *colleague*	i colleghi/le colleghe *colleagues*
l'atleta *athlete*	gli atleti/le atlete *athletes*

■ **3.6.6** A few nouns are always feminine, even when referring to a man:

la persona *person,* la guida *guide,* la vittima *victim*

■ **3.6.7** A few nouns are always masculine, even when referring to a woman:

l'architetto *architect,* l'ingegnere *engineer,*
il medico *doctor,* il ministro *minister,* il soprano *soprano*

■ **3.6.8** When talking about professions, it is now common to use a masculine noun for both men and women, even when a feminine form exists:

La signora Fini è avvocato.	*Mrs Fini is a lawyer.*
Luisa è il direttore del personale.	*Luisa is the personnel manager.*

■ **3.6.9** When grouping males and females, the masculine plural form is used:

figlio *son*	Abbiamo tre figli.	*We have three children.*
fratello *brother*	Hai fratelli?	*Do you have any brothers and sisters?*
zio *uncle*	Gli zii arrivano oggi.	*My uncle(s) and aunt(s) arrive today.*

4 Noun suffixes

Suffixes are endings which can be added to the end of a noun, without its final vowel, to modify its meaning. They are often used instead of adjectives.

They sometimes refer to size, but they can also reflect the user's emotions, conveying affection, goodwill or disgust.

The most common suffixes include:

- **-ino/-ina, -etto/-etta** *little/small*

ragazzo *boy*	Guarda quel ragazzino.	*Look at that sweet little boy.*
isola *island*	Ustica è un'isoletta vicino alla Sicilia.	*Ustica is a small island near Sicily.*

Other suffixes of this type include **-ello**, **-ellino**, **-icello**.

- **-one** *big/great big*

ragazzo *boy*	Sandro è un ragazzone.	*Sandro is a big lad.*
borsa *bag*	Dov'è il borsone?	*Where is the large bag?*

A noun with this suffix is always masculine.

- **-accio/-accia** *bad/horrible*

ragazzo *boy*	Che ragazzaccio!	*What a lout!*
roba *goods/stuff*	È pieno di robaccia.	*It's full of rubbish.*

Another suffix with negative connotations is **-astro**.

Care must be taken when using suffixes:

- not all nouns can be modified
- there are no absolute or consistent rules for their use
- meaning often depends on the context in which the words are used.

The indefinite article:
un uno una un'

In Italian there are four forms of the indefinite article 'a'/'an'. The form depends on the gender of the accompanying noun and on the initial letter of the word which immediately follows the article.

5.1 Masculine

The words for 'a'/'an' when used with masculine nouns are **un** and **uno**:

un before vowels and most consonants:

un aperitivo	*an aperitif*
un bicchiere di vino	*a glass of wine*
un sidro	*a cider*

uno before words beginning with:

z	uno zio	*an uncle*
s + consonant	uno sciroppo	*a syrup*
	uno spuntino	*a snack*
gn	uno gnomo	*a gnome*
ps	uno psicologo	*a psychologist*
x	uno xilofono	*a xylophone*

5.2 Feminine

The words for 'a'/'an' when used with feminine nouns are **una** and **un'**:

una before a consonant:

una birra	*a beer*
una limonata	*a lemonade*
una spremuta d'arancia	*an orange juice*

un' before a vowel:

un'aranciata	*an orange drink*
un'altra birra	*another beer*

5.3 Use of the indefinite article

The indefinite article in Italian is used in much the same circumstances as 'a'/'an' in English.

However, it is omitted in the following circumstances.

■ **5.3.1** It is omitted before nouns denoting occupation, religion, status:

Sono studente.	*I am a student.*
Mio fratello è cuoco.	*My brother is a cook.*
Mia suocera è cattolica.	*My mother-in-law is a Catholic.*
Sono vedova.	*I am a widow.*

... except when there is additional information:

Sono uno studente di lingue.	*I am a language student.*
Mio fratello è un cuoco molto bravo.	*My brother is a very good cook.*

■ **5.3.2** It is omitted before 100 or 1000, and with 'half':

Ci sono cento persone.	*There are a hundred people.*
L'ho detto mille volte.	*I've said it a thousand times.*
un chilo e mezzo di mele	*a kilo and a half of apples*
mezza bottiglia di acqua	*half a bottle of water*

■ **5.3.3** It is omitted after **che** in exclamations:

Che buon'idea!	*What a good idea!*
Che seccatura!	*What a nuisance!*
Che peccato!	*What a pity!*

Indefinite articles

masculine	**un** before vowels and most consonants
	uno before z, s + consonant, **ps**, **gn**, **x**
feminine	**una** before consonants
	un' before vowels

6
The definite article:
il l' lo i gli la le

In Italian there are several words for the definite article 'the'. The form depends on the gender and number of the accompanying noun and on the initial letter of the word which immediately follows the article.

6.1 Masculine

The words for 'the' when used with masculine nouns are **il, l', lo, i, gli.**

il before most singular words:
  il campeggio *the campsite,* il direttore *the manager*

l' before singular words beginning with a vowel:
  l'albergo *the hotel,* l'ufficio *the office*
  l'altro campeggio *the other campsite*

lo before singular words beginning with z, s + consonant, **gn, ps, x:**
  lo zaino *the rucksack,* lo sport *sport,* lo sci *skiing*

i before most plural words:
  i campeggi *the campsites,* i direttori *the managers*

gli before plural words beginning with a vowel or with z, s + consonant, **gn, ps, x:**
  gli alberghi *the hotels,* gli uffici *the offices*
  gli sport *sports,* gli zaini *the rucksacks*

6.2 Feminine

The words for 'the' when used with feminine nouns are **la, l'** and **le:**

la before singular words beginning with a consonant:
  la spiaggia *the beach,* la marea *the tide*

l' before singular words beginning with a vowel:
  l'escursione *the trip,* l'alta marea *high tide*

le before plural words:
  le spiagge *the beaches,* le escursioni *the excursions*
  le alte maree *the high tides*

6.3 Use of the definite article

The definite article is used in Italian as in English, and
also in the following circumstances:

■ **6.3.1** when talking about a person and referring to
them by their title:

La signora Bellofiore non c'è.	*Mrs Bellofiore is not here.*
Vuole parlare con il dottor	*Would you like to speak*
Giannini?	*to Dr Giannini?*

... but not when talking TO a person:
  Buongiorno, signora Bellofiore.
  Arrivederci, dottor Giannini.

■ **6.3.2** with names of:

continents:	l'Europa, l'Australia, l'Asia, l'America
countries:	l'Italia, la Gran Bretagna, il Giappone, gli Stati Uniti
large islands:	la Sardegna, la Sicilia
regions:	la Toscana, l'Umbria, il Lazio

■ **6.3.3** with languages:

Studio l'italiano da sei mesi.	*I've been learning Italian for six months.*

... but it is often omitted after **parlare**:

Parla tedesco?	*Do you speak German?*

■ **6.3.4** with the date:
    il millenovecentonovantacinque *1995*
    il quindici maggio *May 15*   l'otto gennaio *January 8*

■ **6.3.5** with the time:
    È l'una.   *It's one o'clock.*
    Sono le otto.   *It's eight o'clock.*

■ **6.3.6** when expressing possession (see 14):
    La mia casa è molto vecchia.   *My house is very old.*
    Questo è il suo biglietto?   *Is this your ticket?*
    I nostri figli sono in vacanza.   *Our children are on holiday.*

... except when referring to singular members of the family:
    Mio fratello e sua moglie sono *My brother and his wife*
    arrivati.   *have arrived.*

■ **6.3.7** with abstract nouns and nouns used in a general sense:
    La libertà è un diritto.   *Freedom is a right.*
    Prima il dovere poi il piacere. *Business before pleasure.*
    I ragni non mi piacciono.   *I don't like spiders.*

Definite articles

	singular	plural	
masculine	**il**	**i**	before most consonants
	l'	**gli**	before vowels
	lo	**gli**	before z, s + consonant, **ps, gn, x**
feminine	**la**	**le**	before consonants
	l'	**le**	before vowels

7 The definite article after prepositions

When a word for 'the' follows certain prepositions (words like 'at', 'in', 'on'), the two combine to form a single word.

7.1 a, da, di, in, su

All forms of 'the' combine with **a** (*at/to*), **da** (*from*), **di** (*of*), **in** (*in*), **su** (*on*):

	il	lo	la	l'	i	gli	le	
a	al	allo	alla	all'	ai	agli	alle	*at/to the*
da	dal	dallo	dalla	dall'	dai	dagli	dalle	*from the*
di	del	dello	della	dell'	dei	degli	delle	*of the*
in	nel	nello	nella	nell'	nei	negli	nelle	*in the*
su	sul	sullo	sulla	sull'	sui	sugli	sulle	*on the*

Andiamo **allo** zoo.	*We're going **to the** zoo.*
È lontano **dai** negozi.	*It's a long way **from the** shops.*
Ha un elenco **degli** orari di visita?	*Do you have a list **of the** visiting hours?*
Il pranzo è incluso **nel** prezzo.	*Lunch is included **in the** price.*
Sulla pianta è qui.	***On the** map it's here.*

7.2 con

Con (*with*) sometimes combines with **il** and **i** to form **col** and **coi**:

Mia sorella arriva **col** treno di mezzogiorno.	*My sister is arriving **on the** twelve o'clock train.*
Arriverà **coi** regali.	*She'll arrive **with the** presents.*

... but

Viene **con la** guida.	*She's coming **with the** guide.*
Viene **con gli** altri.	*She's coming **with the** others.*

8 The partitive article: del dello dell' dei degli della delle

Partitive articles are used before a noun and correspond to the English words 'some' or 'any'. In Italian they are a combination of **di** and the appropriate definite article (see 6 and 7).

8.1 Masculine

The words for 'some' or 'any' with masculine nouns are **del**, **dell'**, **dello** in the singular and **dei**, **degli** in the plural:

il latte	**del** latte
l'olio	**dell'**olio
lo zucchero	**dello** zucchero
i fagiolini	**dei** fagiolini
gli asparagi	**degli** asparagi
gli zucchini	**degli** zucchini

Vorrei del latte e dello zucchero.	*I'd like some milk and some sugar.*
Avete dell'olio extra vergine?	*Have you any extra virgin oil?*
Mi dà dei fagiolini e degli asparagi.	*I'll have some green beans and some asparagus.*
Avete degli zucchini?	*Have you any courgettes?*

8.2 Feminine

The words for 'some' or 'any' with feminine nouns are **della**, **dell'** in the singular and **delle** in the plural:

la pasta	**della** pasta
l'acqua	**dell'**acqua
le melanzane	**delle** melanzane
le albicocche	**delle** albicocche

Ho comprato dell'acqua minerale.	*I've bought some mineral water.*
Ha della pasta integrale?	*Have you any wholemeal pasta?*
Abbiamo delle buone melanzane.	*We have some good aubergines.*
Avete delle albicocche mature?	*Have you any ripe apricots?*

8.3 Use of the partitive article

Del, dello, dell', della, dei, degli, delle are used to indicate an indeterminate quantity. They correspond to 'some' or 'any' in English, but they are not always used in the same way.

■ **8.3.1** In Italian the word for 'some' may be repeated before each noun in a list:

Vorrei della panna, del formaggio e delle uova.	*I'd like some cream, cheese and eggs.*

... but it is often omitted altogether if quantity is not really relevant:

Per la prima colazione c'è caffè, tè o cioccolata, con pane, burro e marmellata.	*For breakfast, there's coffee, tea or chocolate, with bread, butter and jam.*

■ **8.3.2** It is not used in a negative statement:

Non ho comprato zucchero.	*I haven't bought any sugar.*
Non abbiamo albicocche.	*We don't have any apricots.*
Non c'è panna.	*There is no cream.*

Note: for other ways of translating 'some' or 'any', see 18.

9 Adjectives

Adjectives are words like **piccolo** (*small*), **rosso** (*red*), **importante** (*important*), **inglese** (*English*). They describe nouns and in Italian they agree with the noun they describe. Adjectives generally, though not always, come after the noun.

9.1 Agreement of adjectives

Adjectives are listed in a dictionary in the masculine singular form. In Italian, this ending changes according to whether the noun is masculine or feminine (gender), singular or plural (number). This is called 'agreeing' with the noun.

9.2 Adjectives ending in -o

Adjectives ending in **-o** have four forms: masculine and feminine, in the singular and plural, ending in **-o**, **-a**, **-i**, **-e**.

	masculine	*feminine*
singular	modern**o**	modern**a**
plural	modern**i**	modern**e**

È un albergo modern**o**.	*It's a modern hotel.*
La piscina è modern**a**.	*The pool is modern.*
I bagni sono modern**i**?	*Are the bathrooms modern?*
Ci sono camere modern**e**.	*There are modern bedrooms.*

■ **9.2.1** Spelling notes

- Adjectives ending in **-io** drop one **i** in the masculine plural:
  il vecch**io** palazzo *the old palace*
  i vecch**i** palazzi *the old palaces*

- Most adjectives ending in **-co** and **-go**, e.g. **bianco**, **lungo**, add **h** in the plural to retain the hard **c** or **g** sound:
  vini bian**chi** *white wines*   camicie bian**che** *white shirts*
  lun**ghi** viaggi *long journeys*   lun**ghe** passeggiate *long walks*

- Adjectives ending in **-ico**, e.g. **simpatico**, **magnifico**, do not add **h** in the masculine plural:

  Hai amici simpati**ci**.   *You have nice friends.*
  I fiumi sono magnifi**ci**.   *The rivers are magnificent.*

... but they always add **h** in the feminine plural:

  Le ragazze sono simpati**che**.   *The girls are friendly.*
  Le montagne sono   *The mountains are*
  magnifi**che**.   *magnificent.*

9.3 Adjectives ending in -e

Adjectives ending in **-e** have only two forms, singular and plural, ending in **-e** and **-i**. There is no difference between the masculine and feminine forms.

	masculine	feminine
singular	interessante	interessante
plural	interessanti	interessanti

Il museo è interessant**e**.   *The museum is interesting.*
Che visita interessant**e**.   *What an interesting visit.*
Sono luoghi interessant**i**.   *They are interesting places.*
Le mostre sono interessant**i**? *Are the exhibitions interesting?*

9.4 Adjectives describing more than one noun

Usually, an adjective describing more than one noun:

- has the masculine plural form if at least one of the nouns is masculine:

  La spiaggia e il mare   *The beach and the sea are*
  sono meraviglio**si**.   *wonderful.*

- has the feminine plural form if all the nouns are feminine:

  La spiaggia e la piscina   *The beach and the pool are*
  sono meraviglio**se**.   *wonderful.*

9.5 Position of adjectives

When adjectives and nouns are next to each other, the adjective generally, but not always, goes after the noun:

un viaggio **piacevole**   a pleasant journey

■ **9.5.1** Adjectives which always go AFTER the noun:

- adjectives of colour, shape and nationality:

vini rossi	red wines
un tavolo rotondo	a round table
la cucina italiana	Italian cooking

- adjectives used with an adverb (e.g. 'very', 'too', 'so'):

È un posto molto tranquillo.	It's a very quiet spot.
Ho una casa piuttosto piccola.	I have a rather small house.

■ **9.5.2** Adjectives which usually go BEFORE the noun:

- demonstrative adjectives – **questo** and **quello** (see 13.1):

  Mi piace questa città.   I like this town.

- possessive adjectives – **mio**, **tuo**, etc. (see 14):

  Mia figlia lavora a Londra.   My daughter works in London.

- ordinal numbers – **primo**, **secondo**, etc. (see 28):

  Mi dà un biglietto di   I'd like a second-class ticket.
  seconda classe.

- the following common adjectives:

bello beautiful/nice	**brutto** ugly/horrible
buono good	**cattivo** bad
lungo long	**breve** short
grande big	**piccolo** small
un breve soggiorno all'estero	a short stay abroad
una bella gita	a nice outing

■ **9.5.3** An adjective which normally goes after the noun can be placed before it for emphasis, and vice versa:

un meraviglioso viaggio	*a (truly) marvellous journey*
Che viaggio lungo!	*What a long journey!*

■ **9.5.4** A few adjectives actually change their meaning depending on whether they go before or after the noun:

un grand'uomo *a great man*   un uomo grande *a big man*
la stessa cosa *the same thing*   la cosa stessa *the thing itself*
un vecchio amico/un amico vecchio   *an old/elderly friend*

■ **9.5.5** When two adjectives describe the same noun:

* they can both follow the noun:
  un vino rosso italiano   *an Italian red wine*

* they can be separated by the word **e** (*and*):
  un vino secco e piacevole   *a pleasant dry wine*

* sometimes one adjective is placed before the noun:
  uno squisito vino rosso   *a delicious red wine*

9.6 Irregular adjectives

Irregular adjectives do not follow the patterns shown in 9.2 and 9.3.

■ **9.6.1** Adjectives ending in -ista, e.g., **ottimista** (*optimistic*), **socialista** (*socialist*), **femminista** (*feminist*) have the same form for masculine and feminine singular:

un uomo egoista   *a selfish man*
una donna egoista   *a selfish woman*

They end in **-i** in the masculine plural, and **-e** in the feminine plural:

uomini egoisti *selfish men*, donne egoiste *selfish women*

■ **9.6.2** Some adjectives have only one form:

- adjectives of colour derived from nouns or taken from
  other languages:
  rosa *pink*, viola *violet*, marrone *brown*, nocciola *hazel*,
  turchese *turquoise*, blu *dark blue*, beige *beige*
  Ho comprato un vestito rosa.   *I've bought a pink dress.*
  Le scarpe sono blu.   *The shoes are dark blue.*

- two adjectives together describing colour:
  una sciarpa giallo chiaro   *a pale yellow scarf*
  I piatti sono verde smeraldo.   *The plates are emerald green.*

- the few adjectives ending in -**i**:
  un numero pari   *an even number*
  un numero dispari   *an odd number*
  le case altrui   *other people's houses*

■ **9.6.3 bello, buono, grande, santo**
These adjectives can be used before or after the noun.
After the noun they follow the regular patterns for
adjectives ending in -**o** and -**e**, but when they come before
the noun they have some irregular forms. These forms
depend on the gender of the noun and on its initial letter.

- **Bello** has forms similar to the definite article (see 6):

il	un **bel** sorriso	*a nice smile*
lo	un **bello** scandalo	*a fine scandal*
l'	un **bell'**uomo	*a handsome man*
	una **bell'**isola/una **bella** isola	*a beautiful island*
la	una **bella** giornata	*a lovely day*
i	dei **bei** ricordi	*some wonderful memories*
gli	dei **begli** strumenti	*some fine instruments*
le	delle **belle** notizie	*some good news*
	delle **belle** isole	*some beautiful islands*

  Quello follows a similar pattern (see 13.1.2).

- **Buono** has the following forms in the singular:

  masculine
consonant	un **buon** vino	*a good wine*
vowel	un **buon** odore	*a good smell*
z/s + cons.	un **buono** studente	*a good student*

  feminine
consonant	una **buona** cena	*a good dinner*
vowel	una **buon**'idea	*a good idea*

In practice, **buon** is often used before all masculine singular
nouns and **buona** before all feminine singular nouns:
  un buon studente, una buona idea

- **Grande** has the following forms in the singular:

  masculine
consonant	un **gran** piacere	*a great pleasure*
vowel	un **grand**'errore	*a big mistake*
z/s + cons.	un **grande** spettacolo	*a great show*

  feminine
consonant	una **gran** parte	*a large part*
vowel	una **grand**'avventura	*a big adventure*

It is common to use **grande** instead of **gran** or **grand**':
  un grande piacere, un grande errore
  una grande parte, una grande avventura

- **Santo** after a noun means 'holy'. In front of a noun it
  means 'saint' and has the following forms:

	masculine	*feminine*
consonant	**san** Cristoforo	**santa** Maria
vowel	**sant**'Andrea	**sant**'Angela
s + cons.	**santo** Stefano	

9.7 Adjectives + infinitive

Many adjectives can be followed by the infinitive of a verb

È **difficile** trovare una camera.	*It's difficult to find a room.*
È **possibile** tornare domani?	*Is it possible to go back tomorrow?*
È **necessario** prenotare?	*Is it necessary to book?*

9.8 Adjectives + preposition

Some adjectives are followed by a preposition:

a/ad	Stai **attento al** cane.	*Be careful of the dog.*
	Sono **pronto ad** aiutare.	*I'm willing to help.*
	Siamo **abituati al** sole.	*We are used to the sun.*
	È **bravo a** calcio?	*Is he good at football?*
da	La guida non è **difficile da** capire.	*The guide isn't difficult to understand.*
di	Sono **contento di** vederti.	*I'm pleased to see you.*
	Sono **felice di** fare la sua conoscenza.	*I am happy to meet you.*
	La piazza è **piena di** macchine.	*The square is full of cars.*
	Sono **stanco di** aspettare.	*I'm tired of waiting.*
in	Mia figlia è **brava in** matematica.	*My daughter is good at maths.*
per	Siamo **pronti per** il decollo.	*We are ready for take-off.*

9.9 Adjectives after qualcosa and niente

To say 'something' or 'nothing' + adjective, **di** is needed before the adjective:

Ho visto qualcosa di strano.	*I saw something strange.*
Non è successo niente/nulla di interessante.	*Nothing interesting happened.*

Adverbs

Adverbs are words like **lentamente** (*slowly*),
fortunatamente (*fortunately*), **bene** (*well*), **molto** (*very*),
sempre (*always*). They add to the meaning of verbs,
adjectives or other adverbs.
Unlike adjectives, the endings of adverbs do not change.

10.1 Formation of adverbs

■ **10.1.1** Many adverbs are formed by adding **-mente** to
the feminine singular form of an adjective, i.e. the form
ending in **-a** or **-e**.

adjective	→	feminine →	adverb
rapido *quick*		rapida	rapidamente *quickly*
esatto *exact*		esatta	esattamente *exactly*
elegante *elegant*		elegante	elegantemente *elegantly*
semplice *simple*		semplice	semplicemente *simply*

Adjectives ending in vowel + **le** or vowel + **re** drop the
final **e** before adding **-mente**.

adjective	→	adverb
facile *easy*		facilmente *easily*
notevole *considerable*		notevolmente *considerably*
regolare *regular*		regolarmente *regularly*

■ **10.1.2** A few adverbs are very different from the
corresponding adjective:

adjective	→	adverb
buono *good*		bene *well*
cattivo *bad*		male *badly*
migliore *better*		meglio *better*

10.2 Adjectives and phrases used as adverbs

Where an adverb might be used in English, Italian sometimes uses:

- certain adjectives:

gridare **forte**	*to shout loudly*
andare **piano**	*to go slowly*
parlare **chiaro**	*to speak plainly/clearly*
abitare **lontano**	*to live far away*

- **in modo** + adjective:

in modo elegante	*smartly, elegantly*
in modo appropriato	*appropriately*

- preposition + noun:

arrivare **all'improvviso**	*to arrive unexpectedly*
partire **in fretta**	*to leave hastily/hurriedly*
guidare **con cautela**	*to drive carefully*
lavorare **senza entusiasmo**	*to work unenthusiastically*

10.3 Use of adverbs

Adverbs supply information about verbs, adjectives and other adverbs, by specifying:

- how:

Può parlare **lentamente**?	*Can you speak **slowly**?*
Ha dormito **bene**?	*Did you sleep **well**?*

- to what extent:

Siamo **molto** stanchi.	*We are **very** tired.*
Ho mangiato **troppo**.	*I've eaten **too much**.*

- when:

  Vado **spesso** in Italia. | I **often** go to Italy.

  Attualmente il signor Noto è in vacanza. | **At the present time,** Mr Noto is on holiday.

- where:

  C'è una banca **qui vicino**? | Is there a bank **near here**?

  È **lontano**? | Is it **far**?

10.4 Position of adverbs

Adverbs are generally placed:

- before adjectives and other adverbs:

  Sono **molto** stanco. | I'm very tired.

  È **un po'** tardi. | It's a little late.

  Ho dormito **abbastanza** bene. | I slept quite well.

- after verbs:

  Mangiamo **sempre** alle otto. | We always eat at eight o'clock.

  C'è **solo** questo. | There's only this one.

  Ho cercato **dappertutto**. | I've looked everywhere.

  Abbiamo speso **troppo**. | We have spent too much.

■ **10.4.1** In compound tenses (see 35 and 36), some adverbs referring to time go between **avere/essere** and the past participle:

Ho **già** pagato. | I have already paid.

Abbiamo **sempre** lavorato qui. | We have always worked here.

Non ho **ancora** visto quel film. | I haven't seen that film yet.

Molto, poco, tanto and troppo can be used as adjectives, adverbs or pronouns. They correspond to a variety of English words and expressions.

11.1 As adjectives

Like other adjectives ending in -o they have four forms and agree in gender and number with the noun they refer to.

- masculine singular:

Accetto con **molto** piacere.	*I accept with **much** pleasure.*
Ho **poco** tempo oggi	*I have **little** time today*
perché ho **tanto** lavoro.	*because I have **so much** work.*
Pietro ha **troppo** lavoro.	*Pietro has **too much** work.*

- feminine singular:

Abbiamo **molta** concorrenza.	*We have **a lot of** competition.*
Ho **poca** pazienza.	*I do **not** have **much** patience.*
C'è **tanta** gente e	*There are **so many** people*
troppa confusione.	*and **too much** confusion.*

- masculine plural:

In centro città ho visto **molti** ristoranti ma **pochi** alberghi.	*In the town centre I saw **many** restaurants but **few** hotels.*
Ci sono **tanti** negozi e **troppi** turisti.	*There are **so many** shops and **too many** tourists.*

- feminine plural:

Ho trovato **molte** librerie ma **poche** biblioteche.	*I found **many** bookshops but **few** libraries.*
Ci sono **tante** cose da vedere, ma ci sono **troppe** macchine.	*There are **so many** things to see, but there are **too many** cars.*

11.2 As adverbs

When used as adverbs, **molto**, **poco**, **tanto** and **troppo** are invariable, i.e. the endings do not change.

La pizza è **molto** buona.	*The pizza is **very** good.*
Mangio **molto** a mezzogiorno.	*I eat **a lot** at midday.*
Ho dormito **poco**.	*I did **not** sleep **much**.*
I negozi sono **poco** interessanti.	*The shops are **not very** interesting.*
Questa città mi piace **tanto**.	*I like this town **so much**.*
È **tanto** bella.	*It's **so** beautiful.*
Sono arrivato **troppo** presto.	*I arrived **too** early.*
Ho speso **troppo**.	*I have spent **too much**.*

11.3 As pronouns

The plural words **molti**, **pochi**, **tanti**, **troppi** can be used to refer to people without being specific:

Molti conoscono la sua musica.	***Many people** know his music.*
Pochi l'apprezzano.	***Few** appreciate him.*
Tanti hanno applaudito.	***So many people** applauded.*
Ce ne sono **troppi**.	*There are **too many** of them.*

11.4 un po'

Un po', which is a shortened form of **un poco**, means 'a little' or 'a bit':

un po' più tardi	*a little later/a bit later*

It requires **di** before a noun:

Vorrei **un po' di** vino.	*I'd like **a little** wine.*

12 Comparatives and superlatives

Used with adjectives and adverbs, comparatives express 'as ... as', 'more ...' or 'less ...'. Superlatives express 'the most ...' or 'the least ...'.

The key words in Italian are **più** (*more*) and **meno** (*less*).

12.1 as ... as

Tanto ... quanto and **così ... come** mean 'as ... as':

La camicia è tanto cara quanto il vestito.	*The shirt is as expensive as the dress.*
Non posso andare in Italia così spesso come vorrei.	*I can't go to Italy as often as I would like.*

Tanto or **così** can be omitted, with no change in meaning.

La camicia è cara quanto il vestito.

12.2 more .../less ...

To say 'more ...' or 'less ...', **più** or **meno** is placed before the adjective or the adverb:

Questa giacca è più cara.	*This jacket is more expensive.*
Le scarpe sono meno care.	*The shoes are less expensive.*
Può parlare più lentamente?	*Could you speak more slowly?*
Vado meno spesso in città.	*I go to town less often.*

12.3 than

'Than' is expressed by **di** or **che**.

■ **12.3.1 Di** before numbers, pronouns and nouns (except as used in 12.3.2):

Costa meno di 100.000 lire.	*It costs less than 100,000 lire.*
È più giovane di me.	*She's younger than me.*
Tu esci più spesso di Michele.	*You go out more often than Michele.*
Costa più della giacca.	*It costs more than the jacket.*

■ **12.3.2 Che** in all other cases. This usually means comparison between words or phrases in one category.

- Nouns:

  Ho comprato più cartoline che francobolli.

  I've bought more postcards than stamps.

- Adjectives:

  Il cameriere è più simpatico che efficiente.

  The waiter is more friendly than efficient.

- Adverbs:

  Meglio tardi che mai.

  Better late than never.

- Verbs:

  È più facile sciare che pattinare. *It's easier to ski than to skate.*

- Phrases introduced by prepositions:

  Vado meno spesso in Francia che in Italia.

  I go less often to France than to Italy.

12.4 the most .../the least ...

■ **12.4.1** Adjectives

To say 'the most ...' or 'the least ...' in Italian, the appropriate form of the definite article is used with **più** or **meno**.

Questa maglia è **la più** piccola. *This sweater is the smallest.*

Ho comprato **il** biglietto **meno** caro.

I've bought the least expensive ticket.

■ **12.4.2** Adverbs

To say something is done 'the most ...' or 'the least ...', **il più** or **il meno** is placed before the adverb.

Giorgio guida il più rapidamente.

Giorgio drives the most quickly/the fastest.

12.5 -issimo

■ **12.5.1** The ending **-issimo**, added to an adjective without its final vowel, corresponds to the English 'extremely ...' or 'very ... indeed':

È **caro** il vestito?	*Is the dress expensive?*
È **carissimo**.	*It's very expensive indeed.*
La città è **bella**, vero?	*Isn't the town beautiful?*
È **bellissima**.	*It's extremely beautiful.*
I bambini sono **stanchi**?	*Are the children tired?*
Sì, sono **stanchissimi**.	*Yes, they are very tired indeed.*
Le due chiese sono **antiche** – sono **antichissime**.	*The two churches are old – they are extremely old.*

■ **12.5.2** **-issimo** can be added to a few adverbs:

Lei parla **bene**, parla **benissimo** l'italiano.	*You speak well, you speak Italian extremely well.*
Vai **spesso** a Roma?	*Do you often go to Rome?*
Ci vado **spessissimo**.	*I go there very often indeed.*

A few others add **-mente** to the **-issima** form of the adjective:

Guida **lentissimamente**.	*He drives extremely slowly.*

... but it is more common to use **molto** (*very*) or **assai** (*extremely*):

Ci vado **molto** spesso.	*I go there very often.*
Guida **assai** lentamente.	*He drives extremely slowly.*

12.6 more and more .../less and less ...

To say 'more and more ...' or 'less and less ...' **sempre** is used before **più** or **meno**.

Sono sempre più contenta.	*I am happier and happier.*
Esce sempre meno spesso.	*He goes out less and less often.*

12.7 Irregular comparative and superlative adjectives

The following adjectives have irregular comparative and superlative forms as well as the regular forms **più buono**, **il più piccolo**, etc.

adjective	comparative	superlative
buono *good*	migliore *better*	il migliore *best*
cattivo *bad*	peggiore *worse*	il peggiore *worst*
piccolo *small*	minore *smaller*	il minore *smallest*
grande *big*	maggiore *bigger*	il maggiore *biggest*

Oggi il tempo è migliore di ieri.	*Today the weather is better than yesterday.*
La peggiore squadra è ...	*The worst team is ...*

Minore and **maggiore** are used to talk about age, **più piccolo** and **più grande** to talk about size:

La mia figlia minore ha cinque anni.	*My youngest/smallest daughter is five.*
Queste stanze sono più piccole.	*These rooms are smaller.*

12.8 Irregular comparative and superlative adverbs

adverb	comparative	superlative
bene *well*	meglio *better*	il meglio *best*
male *badly*	peggio *worse*	il peggio *worst*
molto *much*	più/di più *more*	il più *most*
poco *little*	meno/di meno *less*	il meno *least*

Sta meglio oggi.	*He is feeling better today.*
Stanotte ha dormito di più.	*Last night he slept more.*

■ **12.8.1 Possibile** can be added to the superlative:

Mangia il meno possibile.	*She eats as little as possible.*

13 Demonstratives

The main demonstratives are **questo** (*this*) and **quello** (*that*). They can be used with a noun (as adjectives) or on their own (as pronouns).

13.1 questo and quello as adjectives

They always go in front of the noun they describe and, like other adjectives, change their ending to agree with that noun.

■ **13.1.1 Questo** has the same four forms as other adjectives ending in -o:

in questo momento	*at this moment*
questa settimana	*this week*
questi ultimi giorni	*these last few days*
queste due settimane	*these two weeks*

Questo and **questa** can be shortened to **quest'** before a vowel:

Quest'anno non vado in vacanza.	*This year I'm not going on holiday.*
Quest'agenzia è chiusa oggi.	*This agency is closed today.*

■ **13.1.2 Quello** has forms which are similar to the definite article (see 6):

il	**quel** viaggio	*that holiday*
lo	**quello** sciopero	*that strike*
l'	**quell'**albergo	*that hotel*
	quell'agenzia	*that agency*
la	**quella** serata	*that evening*
i	**quei** giorni	*those days*
gli	**quegli** ospiti	*those guests*
le	**quelle** persone	*those people*

13.2 questo and quello as pronouns

When used as pronouns, i.e. without a noun, **questo** and **quello** have the following four forms only:

questo	questa	questi	queste
quello	quella	quelli	quelle

■ **13.2.1 Questo** is often used to introduce someone.

Questa è mia moglie.	*This is my wife.*
Questi sono i miei figli.	*These are my children.*

■ **13.2.2 Questo** and **quello** can be used for comparing and contrasting:

Queste sono le camere – questa è più grande di quella.	*These are the rooms – this one is bigger than that one.*
Prendo quelli in vetrina, non mi piacciono questi.	*I'll take those in the window, I don't like these.*

■ **13.2.3 Qui** and **qua** (*here*) are often used after **questo** for emphasis. Similarly, **lì** and **là** (*there*) can be used after **quello**:

Abbiamo due ascensori – questo qui e quello là in fondo.	*We have two lifts – this one and that one at the end.*
Vorrei delle cartoline. Quanto costano queste? ... e quelle lì?	*I'd like some postcards. How much are these? ... and those?*

13.3 ciò

Ciò is used to express 'this' or 'that' when referring to a whole idea or situation rather than to a specific noun. **Ciò** is singular and invariable.

Ciò mi sorprende.	*That surprises me.*
Ciò non vi riguarda.	*This has nothing to do with you.*

14 Possessives

Possession is expressed in Italian by **di** (*of*), or with possessive adjectives or possessive pronouns like **mio** (*my, mine*), **nostro** (*our, ours*), **loro** (*their, theirs*).

14.1 Expressing possession with di

There is no Italian equivalent of the English ['s] to express possession. **Di** (*of*) is used instead:

la moglie di Paolo	*Paolo's wife (the wife of Paolo)*
la casa di Gina	*Gina's house (the house of Gina)*

When **di** is followed by the definite article, the appropriate form of **del, della, dell'**, etc. is needed (see 7):

l'indirizzo del medico	*the doctor's address*
la macchina della mia amica	*my friend's car*

14.2 Form of possessive adjectives and possessive pronouns

In Italian, possessive adjectives and possessive pronouns are identical in form – **mio** translates both 'my' and 'mine', **suo** 'your' and 'yours', etc.

singular		plural		
masculine	feminine	masculine	feminine	
il mio	la mia	i miei	le mie	*my/mine*
il tuo	la tua	i tuoi	le tue	*your/yours*
il suo	la sua	i suoi	le sue	*his/her/hers/ your/yours*
il nostro	la nostra	i nostri	le nostre	*our/ours*
il vostro	la vostra	i vostri	le vostre	*your/yours*
il loro	la loro	i loro	le loro	*their/theirs*

They agree in gender and number with whatever is possessed, NOT with the possessor.

Roberto guida **la sua** macchina.	*Roberto drives **his** car.*
Paola guida **la sua** macchina.	*Paola drives **her** car.*

- **suo/sua/suoi/sue** can mean 'his', 'her(s)' or 'your(s)' (formal). When they mean 'your' or 'yours' they may be written with a capital letter (see 2.5.1).

14.3 Possessive adjectives

■ **14.3.1** A possessive adjective usually needs a definite article ('the') before it:

La mia macchina è rossa.	*My car is red.*
Il nostro professore è di Roma.	*Our teacher is from Rome.*
Ecco **i loro** indirizzi.	*Here are their addresses.*

■ **14.3.2** The definite article is omitted when referring to an individual member of the family:

mia figlia	*my daughter*
sua moglie	*his wife*
nostro cugino	*our cousin*

... except

- when there is additional information about the person:

la mia figlia maggiore	*my eldest daughter*
la sua seconda moglie	*his second wife*
il nostro cugino americano	*our American cousin*

- with **loro**:

la loro sorella	*their sister*
il loro suocero	*their father-in-law*

■ **14.3.3** The definite article is also omitted in a few idiomatic expressions, when the possessive adjective goes after the noun:

È colpa mia.	*It's my fault.*
Andiamo a casa nostra.	*Let's go to our house.*

■ **14.3.4** Possessive adjectives are used less in Italian than in English. The definite article is used instead, when it is clear who the possessor is.

Il signor Notta è arrivato con la moglie.	*Mr Notta arrived with his wife.*
Mi fa male il ginocchio.	*My knee hurts.*

■ **14.3.5** Possessive adjectives are usually repeated before each noun in a list:

il mio coltello e la mia forchetta   *my knife and fork*

■ **14.3.6** Possessive adjectives can be used with the indefinite article (**un/una**) for a slightly different meaning:

È una mia amica.	*She's a friend of mine.*
	She's one of my friends.
Ho un tuo libro.	*I have a book of yours.*
	I have one of your books.

14.4 Possessive pronouns

■ **14.4.1** Possessive pronouns are used without the noun. The definite article is usually needed:

Ho perduto la mia penna – mi puoi prestare **la tua**?	*I've lost my pen – could you lend me yours?*
I vostri figli sono con **i nostri**.	*Your children are with ours.*

The definite article is often omitted after **essere** when the idea of possession is stressed:

Questa valigia è **mia**.	*This case is **mine** (no-one else's).*
Questa valigia è la mia.	***This** case is mine (not that one).*

■ **14.4.2** The masculine plural form of the possessive pronoun can be used to mean 'family'.

I miei vivono a Napoli.	*My family lives in Naples.*
Anna è andata a trovare **i suoi**.	*Anna has gone to see her family.*

15 Exclamations

Che, quale, quanto and come can all be used in exclamations.

15.1 che

Che (*what/how*) is the most common. It can be used with nouns and adjectives:

Che noia!	*What a bore!/How boring!*
Che stupidi!	*What idiots!/How stupid they are!*
Che bello!	*How lovely!*
Che bella giornata!	*What a lovely day!*

15.2 quale

Quale (*what*), also used with nouns and adjectives, is more literary and less common in everyday speech.

Quale spettacolo!	*What a show!/What a performance!*
Quale sciocchezza!	*What nonsense!*

15.3 quanto

Quanto (*what a lot*) has four forms and agrees with the noun:

Quanto rumore!	*What a lot of noise!*
Quanta gente!	*What a lot of people!*
Quanti turisti!	*What a lot of tourists!*
Quante bugie!	*What a lot of lies!*

Quanto can be used with a verb:

Quanto sei gentile!	*How kind you are!*
Quanto abbiamo mangiato!	*What a lot we've eaten!*

15.4 come

Come (*how*) can be used with a verb:

Come ho fame!	*How hungry I am!*
Come parla bene!	*How well you speak!*
Come siete gentili!	*How kind you are!*

16 Interrogatives

Questions are formed in Italian by using the appropriate tone of voice, by adding a questioning expression such as **vero?** to a statement, or by starting with a question word like **dove?** (*where?*) or **chi?** (*who?*).

16.1 Tone of voice

All that is necessary to make a statement into a question is to make it SOUND like a question. The word order can stay the same. The voice drops at the end of a statement but rises at the end of a question.

C'è una banca nella piazza.	*There's a bank in the square.*
C'è una banca nella piazza?	*Is there a bank in the square?*
È inglese lei.	*She's English.*
È inglese lei?	*Is she English?*

16.2 vero?/non è vero?

Vero? or **non è vero?** can be added to a statement. They correspond to English question tags like 'isn't it?', 'don't we?', 'aren't you?' 'hasn't she?' 'won't they?'.

C'è una banca nella piazza, vero?	*There's a bank in the square, isn't there?*
È inglese lei, non è vero?	*She's English, isn't she?*

16.3 Question words

In Italian, as in English, questions can be introduced by various question words.

■ **16.3.1 come?** *how?*

Come sta?	*How are you?*
Come si chiama?	*What's your name?*
	(i.e. How do you call yourself?)
Come funziona questo?	*How does this work?*
Come si dice ... in italiano?	*How do you say ... in Italian?*

■ 16.3.2 dove? *where?*

Dove sono i negozi?	*Where are the shops?*
Dove posso lasciare questa valigia?	*Where can I leave this case?*
Di dove sei?	*Where are you from?*

Dove drops the e before è:

Dov'è la stazione?	*Where is the station?*

■ 16.3.3 quando? *when?*

Quando possiamo entrare?	*When can we go in?*
Quando arriva il treno da Messina?	*When does the train arrive from Messina?*
Fino a quando resta qui?	*Until when are you staying here?*
Da quando abita a Modena?	*Since when have you lived in Modena?*

■ 16.3.4 perché? *why?*

Perché vai a Milano?	*Why are you going to Milan?*
Perché deve partire?	*Why do you have to leave?*
Perché non andiamo in montagna?	*Why don't we go to the mountains?*

■ 16.3.5 chi? *who?/whom?*

Chi abita qui?	*Who lives here?*
Mi può dire chi abita qui?	*Can you tell me who lives here?*
Chi conosce a Verona?	*Who do you know in Verona?*
A chi parlo?	*Who am I speaking to?*
Con chi andiamo?	*Who are we going with?*
Secondo chi?	*According to whom?*

■ 16.3.6 di chi? *whose?*

Di chi è questo cappotto?	*Whose is this coat?*
Di chi sono questi occhiali?	*Whose are these glasses?*
È di chi la macchina rossa?	*Whose is the red car?*

■ **16.3.7 che?** *what?*

Che posso fare?	*What can I do?*
Che hanno detto?	*What did they say?*

- **Che cosa** is often used instead of **che** to ask 'what?', and in everyday speech the informal **cosa** is also common:

Che cosa ha fatto sabato? ⎫
Cosa ha fatto sabato? ⎭ *What did you do on Saturday?*

Che cosa mangiamo? ⎫
Cosa mangiamo? ⎭ *What shall we eat?*

- **Che** can be used with a noun:

Che tipo di torta desidera?	*What kind of cake would you like?*
Che giornali hai comprato?	*What newspapers have you bought?*

■ **16.3.8 quale?** *which? what?*
Quale, and its plural form **quali**, can be used in two ways:

- with a noun (i.e. as an adjective):

In quale mese?	*In which month?*
Quale camera è la tua?	*Which is your room?*
Quali documenti vuole?	*Which papers do you want?*
Quali regioni conosce?	*Which regions do you know?*

- in place of a noun (i.e. as a pronoun):

Quale preferisce?	*Which (one) do you prefer?*
Quali preferisce?	*Which (ones) do you prefer?*

In the singular **quale** often shortens to **qual** before **è**:

Qual è la più grande regione d'Italia?	*Which is the largest region in Italy?*
Qual è il numero di telefono?	*What is the telephone number?*

■ **16.3.9 quanto?** *how much? how many?*

In questions, **quanto** can be used in three ways:

• with a verb (i.e. as an adverb).

Quanto does not change to agree with any other words in the sentence, but it can shorten to **quant'** before a vowel:

Quanto costa?	*How much does it cost?*
Quanto costano le cartoline?	*How much do the postcards cost?*
Quanto dista da qui?	*How far is it from here?*
Quant'è?	*How much is it?*

• with a noun (i.e. as an adjective).

Used in this way, **quanto** has to agree with the noun. Like other adjectives ending in **-o**, it has four forms:

Quanto tempo abbiamo?	*How much time have we got?*
Quanta birra vuoi?	*How much beer would you like?*
Quanti biglietti hai?	*How many tickets have you got?*
Quante persone ci sono?	*How many people are there?*

• in place of a noun (i.e. as a pronoun).

Used as a pronoun, **quanto** has to agree with the noun it refers to:

Ha comprato vino? Quanto?	*Have you bought any wine? How much?*
Un po' di pizza? Quanta ne vuoi?	*A bit of pizza? How much do you want?*
In quanti siete?	*How many of you are there?*
Delle paste? Quante?	*Some cakes? How many?*

17 Negatives

To make a negative statement, Italian uses **non** (*not*) and negative words like **niente** (*nothing*) or **mai** (*never*). Unlike in English, both **non** and the negative word are very often used in the same sentence.

17.1 non

To make a sentence negative in Italian, **non** is placed before the verb:

Sono italiano.	*I am Italian.*
Non sono italiano.	*I am not Italian.*
Gioca a tennis.	*She plays tennis.*
Non gioca a tennis.	*She doesn't play tennis.*
L'ufficio apre domani?	*Does the office open tomorrow?*
L'ufficio non apre domani?	*Doesn't the office open tomorrow?*

■ **17.1.1** If the verb is in the perfect tense (see 35) or another compound tense (see 36), **non** goes before **avere** or **essere**:

Ho mangiato.	*I ate./I've eaten.*
Non ho mangiato.	*I didn't eat./I haven't eaten.*
È arrivata.	*She arrived./She has arrived.*
Non è arrivata.	*She didn't arrive./She hasn't arrived.*
Avevo finito.	*I had finished.*
Non avevo finito.	*I hadn't finished.*

■ **17.1.2** **Non** normally goes before pronouns:

Si alza presto.	*He gets up early.*
Non si alza presto.	*He doesn't get up early.*
Mi piace l'arte moderna.	*I like modern art.*
Non mi piace l'arte moderna.	*I don't like modern art.*
Lo vedo ogni giorno.	*I see him every day.*
Non lo vedo ogni giorno.	*I don't see him every day.*

17.2 nessuno, niente, nulla

Nessuno means 'nobody' or 'not ... anybody'.
Niente and **nulla** both mean 'nothing' or 'not ... anything', but **niente** is more common than **nulla**.
All three are normally used with **non** in the following order:

non + verb + nessuno/niente/nulla

Non conosco nessuno a Verona.	*I don't know anybody in Verona.*
Anna non capisce niente.	*Anna doesn't understand anything.*
Non vedo nulla.	*I see nothing./I can't see anything.*

With verbs in compound tenses (see 35 and 36), **nessuno**, **niente** and **nulla** go AFTER the past participle.

Non ho visto nessuno.	*I haven't seen anybody.*
Non abbiamo mangiato niente.	*We have eaten nothing.*
Non hanno capito nulla.	*They haven't understood anything.*

■ **17.2.1** **Non** + verb + **nessuno** + noun is a slightly emphatic way of saying 'not ... any'.
In this case **nessuno** is an adjective and must agree with the noun. It is only used with singular nouns and has similar forms to the indefinite article (see 5):

Non abbiamo nessun problema.	*We have no problem(s).*
Non fa nessuno sforzo.	*He is not making any effort.*
Non ho avuto nessuna risposta.	*I didn't get any reply/replies.*
Non mi piace nessun'altra.	*I don't like any other(s).*

The English translation is often in the plural.

■ **17.2.2 Niente** can be used with a noun to mean 'no'.
It is invariable.

Niente zucchero per me.   *No sugar for me.*
Niente notizie.   *No news.*

17.3 Other negative words

The negative words below are also used with **non**.

■ **17.3.1** In simple tenses they follow the same rules as
nessuno, **niente** and **nulla**, i.e. **non** + verb + negative word:

non ... mai *never/not ... ever*
Il treno non è mai in orario.   *The train is never on time.*

non ... ancora *not ... yet*
Non è ancora qui.   *He is not here yet.*

non ... più *no longer/not ... any more*
Non vado più a scuola.   *I don't go to school any more.*

non ... affatto, non ... per niente *not ... at all*
Non è affatto gentile.   *He is not at all kind.*
Questo non mi piace   *I don't like this at all.*
per niente.

non ... neppure, non ... neanche, non ... nemmeno *not even*
Non dirà neppure buongiorno.   *He will not even say hello.*
Non uscivo neanche il sabato.   *I didn't go out even on*
  Saturdays.
Non è nemmeno stanca.   *She is not even tired.*

non ... né ... né *neither ... nor*
Non mangio né carne né   *I don't eat meat or fish./*
pesce.   *I eat neither meat nor fish.*

non ... mica *not really, hardly*
Le mele non saranno mica   *The apples will not really be*
mature.   *ripe.*

■ **17.3.2** With verbs in compound tenses, these negative words generally go BEFORE the past participle:

Non sono mai stato a Capri. *I have never been to Capri.*

Non abbiamo ancora mangiato. *We have not eaten yet.*

Non hanno nemmeno comincito. *They haven't even started.*

... except **né ... né ...** which follows the past participle:

Non ho visto né bar né negozio. *I haven't seen a bar or a shop.*

17.4 Negative words without non

There are cases when **non** is not used in a negative sentence.

- When the negative word begins the sentence:

  Nessuno vuole nuotare. *Nobody wants to swim.*

  Nessuno vuole nuotare? *Doesn't anybody want to swim?*

  Neanche Marco lo sa. *Not even Marco knows.*

- When the negative word stands alone:

  Chi hai visto? Nessuno. *Who did you see? Nobody.*

  Che cosa stai facendo? Niente. *What are you doing? Nothing.*

  Sei stato in Russia? Mai. *Have you been to Russia? Never.*

  Ritornerà qui? Mai più! *Will you come back here? Never again.*

- After **senza** (*without*):

  Sono partiti senza dire niente, e senza ringraziare nessuno. *They left without saying anything, and without thanking anybody.*

18 Indefinites

Indefinite adjectives and pronouns refer to people or things without being specific. They are words like **qualcuno** (*somebody*), **ogni** (*every*), **altro** (*other*).

18.1 Indefinite adjectives

Ogni (*every*), **qualche** (*a few*), **qualsiasi/qualunque** (*any*) are invariable – their endings do not change.

- **Ogni** is followed by a singular noun, or by a number:

Lavora ogni giorno.	*He works every day.*
L'autobus passa ogni dieci minuti.	*The bus comes by every ten minutes.*

- **Qualche** is always followed by a singular noun, even though it corresponds to the English 'a few' or 'some':

Ho comprato qualche regalo.	*I've bought a few presents.*
Ci vado qualche volta.	*I go there sometimes.*

In a question, **qualche** means 'any'.

Ha comprato qualche regalo?	*Have you bought any presents?*

- **Qualsiasi** and **qualunque** both mean 'any' or 'any at all'.

Possiamo mangiare a qualsiasi ora.	*We can eat at any time at all.*
Va bene qualunque colore.	*Any colour will do.*

18.2 Indefinite pronouns

Qualcuno (*someone/somebody*), **qualcosa** (*something*), **ognuno** (*everyone/everybody*), **chiunque** (*anyone/anybody*) are pronouns.

Chiunque può farlo.	*Anybody can do it.*
Ognuno per sé.	*Everyone for himself.*
Qualcuno ha telefonato.	*Somebody phoned.*
Qualcosa è successo.	*Something has happened.*

■ **18.2.1** **Qualcosa** can be followed by:

• **di** + adjective:
  Ho visto qualcosa di strano. *I saw something strange.*
  Hai fatto qualcosa di bello? *Have you done anything nice?*

• **da** + verb:
  Vorrei qualcosa da bere. *I would like something to drink.*
  C'è qualcosa da vedere? *Is there anything to see?*

18.3 Indefinite adjectives and pronouns

Many indefinite words can be used as both adjectives and pronouns. They are words like **alcuno** (*some*), **altro** (*other*), **ciascuno** (*each*), **molto** (*much/many*), **parecchio** (*several*), **poco** (*little/few*), **tanto** (*so/so many*), **troppo** (*too much/too many*), **tutto** (*all/everything*). They agree with the noun.

C'è troppa gente qui.	*There are too many people here.*
Troppi sono venuti.	*Too many people came.*
Ho altre cose da fare.	*I have other things to do.*
Altri sono già partiti.	*Others have already left.*
Alcuni lo conoscono.	*Some people know him.*
Ci è stato alcune volte.	*He's been there a few times.*

■ **18.3.1** **Ciascuno** (*each*) is only used in the singular and has forms similar to the indefinite article (see 5):
  ciascun, ciascuno, ciascuna, ciascun'
  Ciascun libro costa 20.000 *Each book costs 20,000 lire.*
  lire.

■ **18.3.2** When **tutto** (*all/the whole/every*) is used as an adjective, the definite article (see 6) must be included between **tutto** and the noun:
  Ho aspettato tutto il giorno. *I waited all day/the whole day.*
  Tutta la famiglia è qui. *The whole family is here.*
  Lavoro tutti i giorni. *I work every day.*
  Tutte le banche sono chiuse. *All the banks are closed.*

19 Subject pronouns

The subject of a verb indicates who or what is eating, working, hoping, etc. The subject can be a noun, or a subject pronoun which stands instead of the noun.

19.1 Subject pronouns

io	*I*
tu	*you*
lui	*he*
lei	*she*
Lei	*you*
noi	*we*
voi	*you*
loro	*they*

■ **19.1.1** There are three ways of saying 'you' in Italian. The choice depends on who is being addressed:

tu	one person – family, friends, young people, children
Lei	one person – acquaintances, older people
voi	more than one person

- **Lei** meaning 'you' can be written with a capital letter (see 2.5.1). It takes the 3rd person singular form of the verb, i.e. the same form as **lei** (*she*):

  E Lei, dove **abita**?　　　　*And where do you live?*

  Ecco Anna. Dove **abita** lei? *Here is Anna. Where does she live?*

- Adjectives used with **Lei** can be masculine or feminine, depending on the person being addressed:

  Lei è italiano/italiana?　　*Are you Italian?*

- Rarely, and only in very formal situations, **loro** can be used to mean 'you' when addressing more than one person.

19.2 Use of subject pronouns

Subject pronouns are used far less frequently in Italian than in English because the verb ending alone is usually enough to indicate who the subject is. **Arrivano domani** is sufficient to say '**they** arrive tomorrow'.

They are used mainly for:

* clarification:

Come si chiama? can mean 'What's your name?', 'What's his name?' or 'What's her name?'. If it is not obvious from the context who is referred to, the subject pronoun is used:

Come si chiama Lei?	*What's your name?*
Lui, come si chiama?	*What's his name?*

* emphasis:

Io non ci vado.	*I'm not going there.*
Pagano **loro**?	*Are **they** paying?*

* contrast:

Lui beve il vino bianco, ma **lei** preferisce il vino rosso.	*He drinks white wine, but **she** prefers red wine.*

* certain expressions:

Sono io.	*It's me.*
Anche noi.	*So are/did/have/could/we.*
Neanch'io.	*Neither am/have/will/would I.*

19.3 egli, ella, esso, essa, essi, esse

The following subject pronouns exist but are rarely used other than in literary texts:

masculine	feminine
egli *he*	ella *she*
esso *it*	essa *it*
essi *they*	esse *they*

20 Object pronouns

The object of a verb indicates who or what is affected by the verb. The object can be a noun, or a pronoun which stands instead of the noun.

Object pronouns generally go before the verb. There are two kinds – direct, e.g. 'me', 'him', 'them', and indirect, e.g. 'to me', 'to him', 'to them'. The 'to' is often omitted in English.

20.1 Direct and indirect object pronouns

direct		indirect	
mi	me	mi	to me
ti	you	ti	to you
lo	him/it	gli	to him/it
la	her/it/you (formal)	le	to her/it/you (formal)
ci	us	ci	to us
vi	you	vi	to you
li	them (masculine)	gli/loro	to them
le	them (feminine)		

Loro is less common and more formal than **gli**; it goes after the verb.

20.2 1st and 2nd persons

Mi, ti, ci and **vi** act as both direct and indirect object pronouns.

direct	**Mi** conoscono bene.	*They know **me** well.*
indirect	**Mi** dia la valigia.	*Give **me** your case/* *Give your case **to me**.*
direct	**Vi** ringrazio tutti.	*I thank **you** all.*
indirect	**Vi** spedirò i biglietti.	*I'll send **you** the tickets./* *I'll send the tickets **to you**.*

20.3 3rd person

In the 3rd person it is important to distinguish between direct and indirect object pronouns.

direct	Anna **lo/la** odia.	*Anna hates **him/her/it**.*
indirect	Anna **gli/le** parla.	*Anna is talking **to him/to her**.*
direct	**Li/le** vedo bene.	*I can see **them** clearly.*
indirect	**Gli** ho scritto.	*I have written **to them**.*

■ **20.3.1** Lo and la can shorten to l' before a vowel, or before **h**:

L'ammetto volentieri.	*I admit it willingly.*
L'ho vista.	*I have seen her.*

■ **20.3.2** Li is used when 'them' refers to a mixed group of masculine and feminine nouns:

La borsa e il portafoglio sono cari, ma **li** prendo.	*The bag and the purse are expensive, but I'll take **them**.*

■ **20.3.3** Le has three different meanings as a pronoun:

- **le** *them (feminine)*

Che belle scarpe – **le** compro.	*What lovely shoes – I'll buy **them**.*

- **le** *to you (formal)*

Signore, **le** possiamo mostrare la camera.	*We can show **you** the room, sir.*
Le ho scritto.	*I've written **to you**.*

- **le** *to her*

Non **le** ho scritto.	*I haven't written **to her**.*
Domani **le** telefonerò.	*Tomorrow I'll phone **her**.*

■ **20.3.4** **Gli** has two different meanings as a pronoun, '(to) him' or '(to) them':

Gli ho spiegato il problema.	*I have explained the problem to him/to them.*
Gli dica di telefonare.	*Tell him/them to phone.*

If there is any chance of confusion, **loro** can be used instead of **gli** to say 'to them'.

> Ho spiegato **loro** il problema. *I have explained the problem to them.*

■ **20.3.5** **Lo** is often used in Italian to refer to a whole phrase or idea. It is not translated in English, but could be thought of as 'it':

Hanno vinto. – **Lo** so.	*They've won. – I know.*
Dov'è tuo fratello? – Non **lo** so.	*Where's your brother? – I don't know.*
Me **l'**ha detto mia madre.	*My mother told me.*

20.4 Verbs taking direct/indirect objects

Generally, the same verbs take direct or indirect object pronouns in Italian and English. Common exceptions include the following:

- verbs which take an indirect object in Italian:

telefonare	**Gli** telefono subito.	*I'll phone him immediately.*
chiedere	**Le** chiedo un favore.	*I'm asking you a favour.*
piacere	**Gli** piace lo sport.	*He likes sport.*
	Le piacciono i fichi?	*Do you like figs?*

- verbs which take a direct object in Italian:

ascoltare	**Lo** ascolti?	*Are you listening to him?*
aspettare	**Li** aspetto qui.	*I'll wait for them here.*
cercare	**La** cercherò dopo.	*I'll look for her later.*

20.5 Combined object pronouns

When indirect object pronouns are used in the same
sentence as direct object pronouns or **ne** (see 24):

- indirect object pronouns change in form:
  mi, ti, ci, vi → **me, te, ce, ve**
  gli, le → **glie**

- indirect object pronouns go before direct object
  pronouns and **ne**:
  Me lo spediranno?   *Will they send it to me?*
  Ve li mostro subito.   *I will show them to you immediately.*
  Te ne darò domani.   *I'll give you some tomorrow.*

- **glie** combines with **lo, la, li, le, ne** to form one word.
  Le piace questa fotografia? *Do you like this photograph?*
  Allora **gliela** regalo.   *Then I'll give it to you.*
  L'elenco? **Glielo** mostro   *The list? I'll show it to you at*
  subito.   *once.*
  Se Marco ha bisogno di   *If Marco needs some stamps,*
  francobolli, **gliene** posso *I can give him three.*
  dare tre.

	lo	la	li	le	ne
mi	me lo	me la	me li	me le	me ne
ti	te lo	te la	te li	te le	te ne
gli le	glielo	gliela	glieli	gliele	gliene
ci	ce lo	ce la	ce li	ce le	ce ne
vi	ve lo	ve la	ve li	ve le	ve ne
gli	glielo	gliela	glieli	gliele	gliene

20.6 Position of object pronouns

Object pronouns usually go before the verb. However, there are some exceptions to this.

■ **20.6.1** Object pronouns follow an infinitive and are attached to it, without its final **e**:

È difficile veder**lo**.	*It's difficult to see it.*
Bisogna mostrar**glielo**.	*We have to show it to them.*

However, when the infinitive is after **dovere** (*to have to*), **potere** (*to be able to*) or **volere** (*to want to*), there are two possible positions for pronouns. They can either be attached to the infinitive, or go before **dovere**, **potere**, **volere**:

È un buon film, **lo** deve vedere/deve veder**lo**.	*It's a good film, you must see it.*
Mi puoi mandare un fax?⎫ Puoi mandar**mi** un fax? ⎭	*Can you send me a fax?*
Te lo posso mandare subito.⎫ Posso mandar**telo** subito. ⎭	*I can send it to you immediately.*

■ **20.6.2** Object pronouns follow **ecco**, the **tu**, **noi** and **voi** forms of the imperative (see 41), the past participle used alone (see 38.2), and the gerund (see 39), and are attached to them:

Ecco**lo**!	*Here he is!/There he is!*
Aspetta**mi**.	*Wait for me.*
Scriviamo**le**.	*Let's write to her.*
Scusate**mi**.	*Excuse me.*
Trovato**lo**, l'ho comprato.	*Having found it, I bought it.*
Vedendo**la**, ho deciso di aspettare.	*Seeing her, I decided to wait.*

However, they are not usually attached to the gerund when it is used with **stare** (see 30.4):

La sto guardando.	*I am watching her.*

20.7 Stressed object pronouns

When there is a need to stress an object pronoun, the following pronouns are used. They have the same form as subject pronouns (see 19), except for **me** and **te**. They generally come AFTER the verb.

me	*me*	**noi**	*us*
te	*you*	**voi**	*you*
lui	*him*	**loro**	*them*
lei	*her*		
Lei	*you*		

■ **20.7.1** Stressed pronouns are used instead of a direct or an indirect object pronoun:

• to stress or emphasize the pronoun:

Conosco **lei**, ma non conosco **lui**.	*I know **her**, but I don't know **him**.*
Hanno dato la lettera a **me**.	*They gave the letter to **me**.*

• to clarify meaning.

For example, **Gliel'ho dato** can mean 'I gave it to him', 'I gave it to her', 'I gave it to you' or 'I gave it to them'. If the meaning is not obvious from the context, stressed pronouns are used:

L'ho dato **a lui**.   L'ho dato **a lei**.   L'ho dato **a loro**.

■ **20.7.2** Stressed pronouns are also used after prepositions:

a	È seduta accanto a me.	*She is sitting next to me.*
con	Posso venire con voi?	*Can I come with you?*
da	Andiamo da loro.	*Let's go to their house.*
di	Sei più giovane di lei.	*You're younger than her.*
fra	È diviso fra lui e me.	*It's shared between him and me.*
secondo	Secondo te, è buono?	*In your opinion, is it good?*

Reflexive pronouns are an essential part of reflexive verbs (see 43); the plural forms can also be used with other verbs to express 'each other' or 'one another'.

mi	*myself*
ti	*yourself*
si	*himself/herself/itself/yourself (formal)*
ci	*ourselves*
vi	*yourselves*
si	*themselves*

21.1 As part of reflexive verbs

Mi diverto qui.	*I'm enjoying myself here.*
Ti sei lavato?	*Did you wash yourself?*
Si guardano nello specchio.	*They're looking at themselves in the mirror.*
Non si è fatto male.	*He didn't hurt himself.*

They are often not translated in English:

Mi alzo presto.	*I get up early.*
Ti senti meglio?	*Are you feeling better?*
Ci fermiamo qui.	*We're stopping here.*

21.2 each other

The plural pronouns **ci**, **vi**, **si** can be used to convey the idea of 'each other' or 'one another':

Ci vediamo ogni giorno.	*We see each other every day.*
Vi conoscete da molto tempo?	*Have you known each other long?*
Si aiutano molto.	*They help one another a lot.*
Si sono salutati.	*They greeted each other.*

21.3 Use with other pronouns and ne

Mi, ti, si, ci, vi, si change to **me, te, se, ce, ve, se** before
other object pronouns:

Mi tolgo la giacca –	*I'm taking my jacket off –*
me la tolgo.	*I'm taking it off.*
Si ricordano l'indirizzo?	*Do they remember the address?*
– **se lo** ricordano?	*– do they remember it?*
Ti compri del pane?	*Are you buying some bread?*
Sì, **me ne** compro.	*Yes, I'm buying some.*

	lo	la	li	le	ne
mi	me lo	me la	me li	me le	me ne
ti	te lo	te la	te li	te le	te ne
si	se lo	se la	se li	se le	se ne
ci	ce lo	ce la	ce li	ce le	ce ne
vi	ve lo	ve la	ve li	ve le	ve ne
si	se lo	se la	se li	se le	se ne

22 Si

Si can be used as the subject of a verb, and corresponds to several English words – 'one', 'you', 'we', 'they', 'people'. It can also be used with a passive meaning to say that something is done.

Si mangia bene in Italia.	*They/you eat well in Italy.*
Si può parcheggiare qui?	*Can you/one park here?*
Si deve partire subito.	*We must leave straight away.*
Come si scrive?	{*How do you write it?* / *How is it written?*
Qui si parla inglese.	{*They speak English here.* / *English is spoken here.*

22.1 si with a verb and direct object

When there is a direct object after **si** + verb:

- the verb is singular with a singular object:

Si porta un regalo.	*You take a present./A present is taken.*
Si vende il vino.	*They sell wine./Wine is sold.*

- the verb is plural with a plural object:

Si portano dei fiori.	*You take flowers./Flowers are taken.*
Si vendono biglietti qui.	*They sell tickets here./Tickets are sold here.*

22.2 si with essere and an adjective

An adjective used with **si** is masculine plural:

Quando si è vecchi.	*When one is old.*
Si era contenti allora.	*People were happy then.*

22.3 si in compound tenses

In compound tenses (see 35, 36), **si** always takes **essere**:

Si è speso molto.	*People spent a lot./A lot was spent.*
Si era mangiato bene.	*We had eaten well.*

If the verb normally takes **essere** in compound tenses, the past participle is masculine plural:

Si è andati al cinema.	*We went to the cinema.*
Si è arrivati in ritardo.	*People arrived late.*

But with a verb which would normally take **avere** in compound tenses, the past participle is masculine singular:

Si è comprato poco.	*They bought little.*
Si è parlato fino a tardi.	*We talked until late.*

... unless that verb has a direct object, in which case the past participle agrees with it:

Si è comprata la pizza.	*They bought pizza.*
Si sono viste tante belle cose.	*We saw so many beautiful things.*

22.4 si with reflexive verbs

When **si** is used with a reflexive verb, **ci si** is used, to avoid repeating **si**.

Ci si alza tardi.	*People get up late.*
Ci si diverte qui.	*You enjoy yourself here.*
Ci si è divertiti ieri.	*We enjoyed ourselves yesterday.*

22.5 si with other pronouns

An object pronoun goes before **si**:

Lo si scrive così.	*You write it this way./It is written like this.*
La si vede spesso.	*People see her often./She is often seen.*
Gli si scrive spesso.	*People often write to him.*

22.6 si with ne

Ne goes after **si**, which then changes to **se**:

Se ne parla molto.	*It is talked about a lot.*
Se ne compra tanto.	*People buy so much of it.*

Ci, which generally comes before the verb, has several meanings. In certain circumstances it changes to ce

23.1 us/to us

In this case, ci is an object pronoun (see 20.1).

Ci hanno invitato.	*They have invited us.*
Ci può dire dov'è il centro?	*Can you tell us where the centre is?*
Non ci scrive spesso.	*She doesn't write to us often.*

23.2 ourselves/each other

(See 21.1 and 21.2.)

Ci divertiamo qui.	*We're enjoying ourselves here.*
Ci siamo alzati alle otto.	*We got up at 8 o'clock.*
Ci vediamo ogni tanto.	*We see each other now and then.*

23.3 there

Ci sono molte trattorie.	*There are many restaurants.*
Vai a Roma? Ci vado domani.	*Are you going to Rome? I'm going there tomorrow.*
C'è una banca in via Gramsci?	*Is there is a bank in via Gramsci?*

(C'è = Ci + è)

23.4 ci instead of phrases introduced by a

Ci can replace a phrase introduced by a:

Penso **al mio lavoro**, ci penso molto.	*I think about my work, I think about it a lot.*
Credo **agli oroscopi**, ci credi tu?	*I believe in horoscopes, do you believe in them?*
È riuscito **a trovare l'indirizzo**? No, non **ci** sono riuscito.	*Did you manage to find th address? No, I didn't.*

23.5 ci after the verb

Although **ci** usually goes before the verb, it goes at the
end of infinitives (without the final **e**), imperatives
(see 41) and gerunds (see 39):

Basta scriver**ci**.	*Just write to us.*
Quando possiamo riveder**ci**?	*When can we see each other again?*
È inutile rimaner**ci**.	*It's no use staying here.*
Andiamo**ci**.	*Let's go there.*
Scriviamo**ci**.	*Let's write to each other.*
Pensando**ci**, ho cambiato idea.	*Thinking about it, I've changed my mind.*

23.6 ci with other pronouns and ne

Ci changes to **ce** when there is an object pronoun or **ne** in
the same sentence.

Vuole mettere il vino nel frigo? **Ce lo** mette Anna.	*Would you put the wine in the fridge? Anna will put it there.*
C'è una farmacia qui? **Ce n'**è una in centro città. (Ce n'è = Ce + ne + è)	*Is there a chemist here? There's one in town.*

23.7 ci in colloquial phrases

Ci (or **ce**) is used in several colloquial phrases, without a
direct translation:

Ce l'hai la chiave?	*Have you got the key?*
Sì, ce l'ho in tasca.	*Yes, I've got it in my pocket.*
Ci vuole pazienza.	*One needs patience.*
Ci vogliono dieci minuti.	*It takes ten minutes.*
Non ce la faccio.	*I can't manage.*
Non ci capisco niente.	*I don't understand a thing.*

24 Ne

Ne, which generally comes before the verb, has several meanings. It is often not translated in English, but it cannot be omitted in Italian.

24.1 ne in phrases of quantity

Ne corresponds to the English 'of it', 'of them', 'some', 'any', in phrases involving quantities:

Hai dei soldi? – Ne ho.	*Have you any money? – I have*
Non ne ho.	*some. I don't have any.*
Questo vino è buonissimo,	*This wine is excellent,*
ne vuoi?	*would you like some (of it)?*
Quanto formaggio vuole?	*How much cheese would*
Ne prendo due etti.	*you like? I'll take 200 grams*
	(of it).
Avete figli?	*Do you have any children?*
Ne abbiamo tre.	*We have three (of them).*

24.2 ne instead of phrases introduced by di

Ne can replace a phrase introduced by **di**:

Non parla **di sua sorella**.	*He doesn't talk about his sister.*
Non **ne** parla.	*He doesn't talk about her.*
Sei sicuro **del numero**?	*Are you sure of the number?*
Ne sei sicuro?	*Are you sure of it?*
Ha bisogno **di una**	*Do you need a pen?*
penna? Sì, **ne** ho bisogno.	*Yes, I need one.*

24.3 ne after the verb

Although **ne** usually goes before the verb, it goes at the end of infinitives (without the final **e**), imperatives (see 41) and gerunds (see 39):

Vorrei assaggiar**ne**.	*I'd like to taste some.*
Compriamo**ne**.	*Let's buy some of it/of them.*
Assaggiando**ne**, mi è piaciuto.	*On tasting some, I liked it.*

24.4 ne + past participle

When **ne** is used with a verb which takes **avere** in compound tenses (see 35.5):

- the past participle has to agree with what **ne** stands for, when talking about quantities:

Vuoi dell'acqua minerale? **Ne** ho compr**ata** una bottiglia.	*Would you like some mineral water? I've bought a bottle.*
Zucchini? **Ne** ho compr**ati** un chilo.	*Courgettes? I bought a kilo.*

- the past participle does not agree when **ne** replaces a phrase introduced by **di** (see 24.2):

Non ha parlato di sua sorella.	*He didn't talk about his sister.*
Non **ne** ha parlato.	*He didn't talk about her.*

24.5 ne with other pronouns

Ne comes after an object pronoun or a reflexive pronoun, except in the case of **loro**.

Me ne comprerà una.	*She'll buy me one (of them).*
Gliene regalo una bottiglia.	*I'll give you a bottle (of it).*
Mi occupo dei bagagli, **me ne** occupo.	*I'm dealing with the luggage, I'm dealing with it.*
Ne parlerò **loro**.	*I'll talk to them about it.*

24.6 andarsene

Ne is an essential part of the verb **andarsene** (*to go away*):

Me ne vado domani.	*I'm going away tomorrow.*
Se ne sono andati.	*They've gone away.*
Devo andarmene.	*I have to go.*
Vattene!	*Go away!*

25 Relative pronouns

Relative pronouns are words like **che** or **cui** – 'who', 'whom', 'which', 'that'. They relate to a noun earlier in the sentence and introduce more information about that noun.

In Italian, relative pronouns are used consistently, and cannot be omitted as often happens in English.

25.1 che

Che corresponds to 'who', 'whom', 'which', 'that', and is used for both people and things.

La donna che lavora nel negozio.	*The woman who works in the shop.*
I cugini che ho visto ieri.	*The cousins (whom) I saw yesterday.*
La macchina che voglio noleggiare.	*The car (which) I want to hire.*
L'orologio che ho comprato non funziona.	*The watch (that) I bought doesn't work.*

25.2 cui

Cui is used instead of **che** after prepositions.

La donna **con cui** lavoro.	*The woman I work with. (The woman with whom I work.)*
I cugini **a cui** ho parlato.	*The cousins I spoke to. (The cousins to whom I spoke.)*
La macchina **in cui** siamo andati a Napoli.	*The car we went to Naples in. (The car in which we went to Naples.)*
Questo è l'orologio **di cui** parlavo.	*This is the watch I was talking about. (This is the watch about which I was talking.)*

25.3 il quale

Il quale, **la quale**, **i quali**, **le quali**, which agree with the noun they relate to, can be used instead of **che**.

La donna **la quale** lavora nel negozio.	*The woman who works in the shop.*
I cugini **i quali** sono partiti ieri.	*The cousins who left yesterday.*

They can also be used instead of **cui** after prepositions.
Il, **la**, **i** and **le** combine with some prepositions (see 7):

La donna **con la quale** lavoro.	*The woman I work with.*
Questo è l'orologio **del quale** parlavo.	*This is the watch I was talking about.*

There is no difference in meaning between **che** and **quale**, but **quale** is less common, and tends to be used where **che** might be ambiguous.

La figlia di Sergio, **la quale** abita qui.	*Sergio's daughter, who lives here.*
La figlia di Sergio, **il quale** abita qui.	*The daughter of Sergio who lives here.*

25.4 il cui

Il cui, **la cui**, **i cui**, **le cui** correspond to 'whose':

La donna **il cui** figlio lavora nel negozio.	*The woman whose son works in the shop.*
La persona **i cui** cugini sono venuti ieri.	*The person whose cousins came yesterday.*

25.5 il che

Il che is used to translate 'which' when it represents a whole idea, not just a specific noun.

Lucia è arrivata, il che mi sorprende.	*Lucia has arrived, which surprises me.*

26 Prepositions

Prepositions are words like **di** (*of*), **con** (*with*), **fra** (*between*), which are followed by a noun or a pronoun, an infinitive or a gerund. Italian and English prepositions often do not correspond in meaning or usage.

A, da, di, in, su combine with a following definite article (see 7).

26.1 a

A sometimes becomes **ad** before a vowel, especially an 'a'.

■ **26.1.1** to – a person:

Scrivo **a** mio fratello.	*I'm writing to my brother.*
Ha dato l'assegno **al** padrone.	*He gave the cheque to the owner.*

■ **26.1.2** to, at, in – a place:

Vai **al** cinema?	*Are you going to the cinema?*
Vado **a** Siena domani.	*I'm going to Siena tomorrow.*
Siamo **a** casa.	*We are at home.*
Abito **ad** Arezzo.	*I live in Arezzo.*
Il mio amico lavora **a** Capri.	*My friend works in Capri.*

... but **in** is used with regions, countries, large islands, continents (see 26.4.2).

■ **26.1.3** at – with expressions of time:

A che ora parte il treno?	*(At) what time does the train leave*
Parte **alle** sette.	*It leaves at seven o'clock.*
Arriva **a** mezzogiorno.	*It arrives at noon.*
Mangiamo **all**'una.	*We eat at one o'clock.*
a Natale	*at Christmas*
a vent'anni	*at twenty (when I was twenty)*

■ **26.1.4** until:

da martedì **a** giovedì	*from Tuesday until Thursday*
dalle nove **alle** undici	*from nine till eleven o'clock*
A domani!	*See you tomorrow!*
Alla settimana prossima!	*See you next week!*

■ **26.1.5** per:

Costano mille lire **al** chilo.	*They cost a thousand lire per kilo.*
Costa 2.500 lire **all'**etto.	*It costs 2,500 lire per 100 grams.*

■ **26.1.6** in expressions giving direction, distance, location:

Prenda la prima **a** sinistra.	*Take the first on the left.*
Gli scavi sono **a** due chilometri.	*The excavations are two km away.*
È **a** cinque minuti dall'albergo.	*It is five minutes away from the hotel.*
Perugia è **a** nord di Roma.	*Perugia is north of Rome.*

■ **26.1.7** in many expressions relating to food and drink:

fegato **alla** veneziana	*liver, Venetian style*
spaghetti **alle** vongole	*spaghetti with clams*
lasagne **al** forno	*baked lasagne*
tè **al** limone	*lemon tea*

■ **26.1.8** after certain adjectives:

Sei bravo **a** tennis?	*Are you good at tennis?*
Siamo pronti **ad** uscire.	*We're ready to go out.*
Attento **a** non perderti!	*Be careful not to get lost!*
Sono abituato **alla** pioggia.	*I'm used to the rain.*

■ **26.1.9** after certain verbs (see 46.1, 46.2, 46.5):

Andiamo **a** vedere.	*Let's go and see.*
Comincia **a** piovere.	*It's starting to rain.*
Continua **a** fare caldo.	*It's still hot.*
Ho telefonato **a** Luisa.	*I phoned Luisa.*

26.2 da

■ 26.2.1 from – time and place:

da lunedì a venerdì	*from Monday to Friday*
dal 17 al 27 maggio	*from the 17th to the 27th of May*
Vengono **da** Siracusa oggi.	*They're coming from Siracusa today.*
L'albergo è lontano **dal** centro.	*The hotel is far from the centre.*
Quanto dista **da** Verona?	*How far is it from Verona?*

■ 26.2.2 by:

È scritto **da** Moravia.	*It is written by Moravia.*
La torta è stata fatta **da** mia madre.	*The cake was made by my mother*

■ 26.2.3 since/for:

Imparo l'italiano	*I have been learning Italian*
... **da** settembre.	*... since September.*
... **da** sei mesi.	*... for six months.*
Abito qui **dal** 1987.	*I have been living here since 1987*
Da quanto aspetti?	*How long have you been waiting (for)?*

■ 26.2.4 ...'s house/place:

Mangiamo **da** mia cugina.	*We're eating at my cousin's.*
Andiamo **da** Giovanna.	*Let's go to Giovanna's.*
Da noi è diverso.	*In our house/country it's different.*
Vado **dal** dentista.	*I'm going to the dentist's.*
L'ho comprato **dal** macellaio.	*I bought it at the butcher's.*

■ **26.2.5** as a ...

Da giovane, lui era molto sportivo.	*As a young man, he was very athletic.*
Da studente mi piaceva il jazz.	*As a student, I liked jazz.*
Da bambina, avevo un cane grande.	*When I was a child I had a big dog.*
Che cosa farai **da** grande?	*What are you going to do when you grow up?*
È vestito **da** soldato.	*He is dressed as a soldier.*
Lo farò **da** solo/**da** sola.	*I'll do it alone.*

■ **26.2.6** to indicate price/value/specification:

un francobollo **da** 900 lire	*a 900 lire stamp*
il menù **da** 60.000 lire	*the 60,000 lire menu*
una pellicola **da** 24 pose	*a 24 exposure film*

■ **26.2.7** to indicate purpose:

- with a noun:

occhiali **da** sole	*sunglasses*
un bicchiere **da** vino	*a wine glass* (NOT *a glass of wine*)
scarpe **da** tennis	*tennis shoes*
un orologio **da** uomo	*a man's watch*

- with an infinitive:

una villa **da** affittare	*a villa to let*
Qualcosa **da** bere, signore?	*Something to drink, sir?*
Cosa c'è **da** vedere qui?	*What is there to see here?*

■ **26.2.8** with personal characteristics:

la donna **dagli** occhi scuri	*the woman with the dark eyes*
l'uomo **dalla** barba grigia	*the man with the grey beard*
la bambina **dai** capelli lunghi	*the child with the long hair*

26.3 di

■ 26.3.1 of:

un bicchiere **di** vino	a glass of wine
un chilo **di** pomodori	a kilo of tomatoes
un po' **di** formaggio	a bit of cheese
un bambino **di** cinque anni	a child of five
ciascuno **di** noi	each of us

■ 26.3.2 (made) of:

una borsa **di** pelle	a leather bag
una camicia **di** seta	a silk shirt
È **di** lana?/**di** legno?	Is it wool?/wood?

■ 26.3.3 (created) by:

un libro **di** Sciascia	a book by Sciascia
un film **di** Fellini	a film by Fellini

■ 26.3.4 some/any (see 8):

Vorrei **del** latte e **della** panna.	I'd like some milk and some cream.
Avete **delle** camere?	Do you have any rooms?
Ho visto **dei** bei monumenti.	I saw some fine monuments.

■ 26.3.5 than – with numbers, pronouns, nouns (see 12.3)

Ho meno **di** 50.000 lire.	I have less than 50,000 lire.
Gioca meglio **di** me.	You play better than I do.
Sei più snella **di** Elisabetta.	You are slimmer than Elisabet

■ 26.3.6 in – after superlatives:

Sei l'uomo più gentile **del** mondo.	You are the kindest man in t| world.
È la più grande regione **d**'Italia.	It's the largest region in Italy.

■ **26.3.7** to denote origin:

Di dov'è?	*Where are you from?*
Sono **di** Milano.	*I'm from Milan.*

■ **26.3.8** to denote possession (see 14.1):

la casa **di** mia madre	*my mother's house*
la figlia **del** ragioniere	*the accountant's daughter*
Di chi è quella macchina?	*Whose is that car?*

■ **26.3.9** replacing ['s] in other circumstances:

l'arrivo **del** treno	*the train's arrival*
il giornale **di** oggi	*today's paper*

■ **26.3.10** forming an adjective.
In English, the first of two nouns next to each other can act as an adjective. In Italian this is not possible.

il numero **di** telefono	*the telephone number*
una torta **di** mele	*an apple pie*
la buccia **di** limone	*lemon peel*

■ **26.3.11** after certain adjectives:

Siamo **contenti di** rivederla.	*We're pleased to see you again.*
Sono **stanco di** lavorare.	*I'm tired of working.*
Antonio è **sicuro di** venire.	*Antonio is sure he'll come.*

■ **26.3.12** after certain verbs (see 46.3, 46.4, 46.5):

Spero di andare a Venezia.	*I hope to go to Venice.*
Abbiamo deciso di rimanere.	*We've decided to stay.*
Ho bisogno dell'indirizzo.	*I need the address.*

■ **26.3.13** with expressions of time (see also 26.4.3):

alle sette **del** mattino	*at seven in the morning*
alle tre **del** pomeriggio	*at three in the afternoon*
alle sette **di** sera	*at seven in the evening*
È chiuso **d'**inverno/**d'**estate.	*It's closed in winter/in summer.*

26.4 in

■ **26.4.1** in/into/to – place:

Palermo è **nel** nord della Sicilia.	Palermo is in the north of Sicily.
I libri sono **nell'**armadio.	The books are in the cupboard.

The definite article is often omitted with familiar places:

Abbiamo una casa **in** campagna.	We have a house in the country.
Vado **in** città.	I'm going into town.
Devo andare **in** banca.	I must go to the bank.

■ **26.4.2** in/to – continents, countries, large islands, regions:

in Europa	in Europe
Siamo andati **in** Australia.	We went to Australia.
Vengono molti turisti **in** Italia.	Many tourists come to Italy.
Abita **in** Sardegna.	He lives in Sardegna.

- Masculine countries may have the definite article after **in**, but it is often omitted in the singular:

Abito **nel/in** Galles.	I live in Wales.
Studia **nel/in** Portogallo.	He is studying in Portugal.
Andiamo **negli** Stati Uniti.	We're going to the USA.

■ **26.4.3** in – time, with years, months, seasons:

Ci sono andato **nel** 1995.	I went there in 1995.
Prendo le vacanze **in** agosto.	I take my holidays in August.
in primavera/**in** autunno	in spring/in autumn
in estate/**in** inverno	in summer/in winter

■ **26.4.4** by – means of transport:

Viaggia **in** aereo/**in** treno.	He's travelling by plane/train.
... **in** barca/... **in** bicicletta	... by boat/... by bike
... **in** corriera/... **in** macchina	... by coach/... by car

26.5 per

■ **26.5.1** for:

Vorrei noleggiarlo **per** un'ora.	I'd like to hire it for an hour.
Siamo rimasti **per** dieci giorni.	We stayed for ten days.
Dobbiamo esserci **per** le otto.	We must be there for eight.
Sarà pronto **per** stasera?	Will it be ready by tonight?
Lavora **per** la Fiat.	He works for Fiat.
Ho comprato dei fiori **per** Anna.	I've bought flowers for Anna.
Partiamo domani **per** la Svizzera.	We leave tomorrow for Switzerland.

■ **26.5.2** in order to + infinitive. This indicates purpose and is often translated as 'to' in English.

Torno a Ravenna **per** vedere i mosaici.	I'm going back to Ravenna (in order) to see the mosaics.
Sono venuto **per** parlarvi.	I've come to talk to you.
Sei troppo giovane **per** uscire da solo.	You're too young to go out alone.

■ **26.5.3** through/along:

Sono passato **per** Catania.	I passed through Catania.
Camminava **per** strada.	He was walking along the street.
L'ho visto **per** strada.	I saw him in the street.

■ **26.5.4** through – because of/from:

Piangeva **per** paura.	She was crying through fear.
Tremeva **per** il freddo.	She was shivering from the cold.

■ **26.5.5** in certain expressions:

per favore/**per** piacere/**per** cortesia	please
il dieci **per** cento	ten per cent
dieci **per** due	ten times two
per posta/**per** via aerea	by post/by air
per terra	on the floor

26.6 su

■ 26.6.1 on:

È seduta **su** una sedia.	*She is sitting on a chair.*
Il giornale è **sul** tavolo.	*The paper is on the table.*
un libro **sulla** guerra	*a book on (about) the war*
su richiesta	*on request*
È salito **sul** treno.	*He got on/into the train.*

■ 26.6.2 over:

Il ponte **sul** fiume Po.	*The bridge over the River Po.*
C'è nebbia **sulla** città.	*There's fog over the town.*

■ 26.6.3 in certain expressions:

sul giornale	*in the paper*
sul momento/**sull**'istante	*there and then*
Il balcone dà **sul** mare.	*The balcony overlooks the sea.*
Ha fatto errore **su** errore.	*He made mistake after mistake.*
nove volte **su** dieci	*nine times out of ten*

■ 26.6.4 Su can also be an adverb, meaning 'up':

Su le mani!	*Hands up!*
Su e giù.	*Up and down.*
Ho guardato in **su**.	*I looked up.*

26.7 fra/tra

Fra and tra are interchangeable.

■ 26.7.1 between/among:

Fra/tra gli ospiti c'è Sofia.	*Among the guests is Sofia.*
È arrivata **fra/tra** le due e le tre.	*She arrived between two and three.*

■ 26.7.2 in – time to come:

Parto **fra/tra** una settimana.	*I'm leaving in a week.*

26.8 Other prepositions

Most other prepositions, such as **con** (*with*), **durante** (*during*), **attraverso** (*through*), **sotto** (*under*), correspond to their English equivalent. Some prepositions need **a** or **di**.

■ **26.8.1** Prepositions with **a** or **di**:

a	accanto a	*next to*
	davanti a	*in front of*
	fino a	*until, as far as*
	di fronte a	*opposite*
	insieme a	*together with*
	intorno a	*around*
	vicino a	*near*
di	invece di	*instead of*
	prima di	*before (time)*

Si trova accanto alla banca.	*It's next to the bank.*
Continui fino al semaforo.	*Go on as far as the traffic lights.*
Parto prima di mezzogiorno.	*I'm leaving before midday.*

■ **26.8.2** The following need **di** before a personal pronoun:

contro	*against*	presso	*near, c/o*
dentro	*inside*	senza	*without*
dietro	*behind*	sopra	*above*
dopo	*after*	sotto	*beneath*

Sono arrivata dopo di loro.	*I arrived after them.*
È partito senza Alfredo e senza di me.	*He left without Alfredo and without me.*

• **Oltre** (*besides*) requires **a** before a personal pronoun:

oltre a noi	*besides us*

27 Cardinal numbers

27.1 0–20

0	zero		
1	uno	11	undici
2	due	12	dodici
3	tre	13	tredici
4	quattro	14	quattordici
5	cinque	15	quindici
6	sei	16	sedici
7	sette	17	diciassette
8	otto	18	diciotto
9	nove	19	diciannove
10	dieci	20	venti

■ **27.1.1** **Zero** translates 'zero', 'nought', 'nil' and 'O' in telephone numbers. It has a plural – **zeri**.

due zeri *two noughts*

■ **27.1.2** **Uno** is the only number which changes to agree with a noun. It has the same forms as the indefinite article 'a'/'an' (see 5):

Ho solo una sorella. *I have only one sister.*

27.2 20–100

20	venti	25	venticinque
21	ventuno	26	ventisei
22	ventidue	27	ventisette
23	ventitré	28	ventotto
24	ventiquattro	29	ventinove

30	trenta	70	settanta
40	quaranta	80	ottanta
50	cinquanta	90	novanta
60	sessanta	100	cento

The numbers 31–99 repeat the pattern of 21–29:

48 quarantotto, 75 settantacinque, 99 novantanove

■ **27.2.1** Numbers are written as one word, unlike English.

- **Venti**, **trenta**, **quaranta**, etc. drop the final vowel before **uno** and **otto**:
  31 trentuno, 58 cinquantotto

- **Ventuno**, **trentuno**, etc. drop the final **o** before a noun:
  Sono rimasto ventun giorni.   *I stayed for 21 days.*

- **Tre** has a written accent when added to another number:
  83 ottantatré

■ **27.2.2** **-ina** can be added to **venti**, **trenta**, **quaranta**, etc. without the final letter. The resulting **ventina**, **trentina**, etc. convey an approximate rather than a precise number. They require **di** when followed by a noun:

Ho letto una trentina di pagine. *I've read about thirty pages.*
Eravamo una cinquantina.   *There were about fifty of us.*

27.3 100 +

100	cento	150	centocinquanta
101	centouno	200	duecento
102	centodue	500	cinquecento
110	centodieci		

1000	mille	10 000	diecimila
1100	millecento	100 000	centomila
1500	millecinquecento	500 000	cinquecentomila
1999	millenovecentonovantanove		

1 000 000	un milione
2 000 000	due milioni
1 000 000 000	un miliardo

■ **27.3.1 Cento** (*a hundred*) is invariable, i.e. it does not change in the plural. **Centinaio** means 'about a hundred'. The plural is **centinaia** (*hundreds*):

Un centinaio di persone sono venute.	*About a hundred people came.*
Alla partita c'erano centinaia di tifosi.	*There were hundreds of fans at the match.*

■ **27.3.2 Mille** (*a thousand*) changes to **mila** in the plural. **Migliaio** means 'about a thousand'. The plural is **migliaia**:

Abbiamo un migliaio di clienti.	*We have about a thousand customers.*
Ogni anno migliaia di turisti visitano la Sardegna.	*Every year thousands of tourists visit Sardinia.*

■ **27.3.4 Un milione** (*a million*) and **un miliardo** (*a billion*) are followed by **di** when used with a noun:

cinque milioni di sterline	*five million pounds*
sette miliardi di lire	*seven billion lire*

■ **27.3.5** A full stop (**punto**) or a space is used to separate thousands, especially over ten thousand:

    24.000   24 000

A comma (**virgola**) is used to indicate a decimal point:

    7,5 sette virgola cinque   0,4 zero virgola quattro

Ordinal numbers are first, third, eighteenth, etc.

28.1 Formation of ordinal numbers

1st to 10th have special forms, but from 11 onwards, ordinal numbers are formed by dropping the final vowel of the cardinal number (see 27) and adding **-esimo**:

1st	primo	1°	11th	undicesimo	11°
2nd	secondo	2°	12th	dodicesimo	12°
3rd	terzo	3°	20th	ventesimo	20°
4th	quarto	4°	30th	trentesimo	30°
5th	quinto	5°	100th	centesimo	100°
6th	sesto	6°			
7th	settimo	7°			
8th	ottavo	8°			
9th	nono	9°			
10th	decimo	10°			

The **tré** of 23, 33, 43, etc. loses the written accent:

23rd ventitreesimo

28.2 Use of ordinal numbers

■ **28.2.1** Ordinal numbers are adjectives. In Italian they agree with the noun and usually go before the noun.

il quinto capitolo	*the fifth chapter*
seconda classe	*second class*
i primi mesi	*the first months*

■ **28.2.2** To say the date in Italian, ordinal numbers are only used for the first day of the month. Cardinal numbers are used for all the other days:

il primo novembre	*1st November*
il dodici gennaio	*12th January*
il ventidue agosto	*22nd August*

29 Verbs

Verbs are words like **mangiare** (*to eat*), **partire** (*to leave*), **pensare** (*to think*), **avere** (*to have*), **essere** (*to be*), which involve DOING or BEING.

29.1 The infinitive

The infinitive of a verb is the basic form found in a dictionary. In Italian, the infinitive ends in **-are**, **-ere** or **-ire**, whereas an English infinitive has the word 'to' before it:

arrivare	*to arrive*
permettere	*to permit*
finire	*to finish*

29.2 Verb stem and endings

When **-are**, **-ere**, **-ire** are removed from the infinitive, the stem of the verb is left.

infinitive	*stem*
arrivare	arriv–
permettere	permett–
finire	fin–

Various endings can then be added to the stem. These verb endings convey information about WHO or WHAT is doing something (person) and WHEN it is done (tense).

arriv**o**	*I arrive*
permett**eva**	*he/she used to permit*
fin**iranno**	*they will finish*

29.3 Person

The person of a verb indicates who or what is doing something. A verb has three persons in the singular and three in the plural:

1st person singular	io	*I*
2nd person singular	tu	*you (familiar)*
3rd person singular	lui/lei/Lei	*he/she/it/you (formal)*
1st person plural	noi	*we*
2nd person plural	voi	*you (plural)*
3rd person plural	loro	*they*

- Verbs are set out in this order, and each group of verbs has a specific ending for the six persons in the various tenses.

- Since verb endings alone are enough to tell us who is arriving, permitting, finishing, etc., subject pronouns, e.g. **io**, **tu**, **noi**, are usually omitted. See 19.2 for guidelines on when to use them.

- The 3rd person singular ending is used for **Lei** (formal 'you') as well as for 'he', 'she' and 'it'.

29.4 Tense

The tense of a verb indicates when something is done – in the past, present or future. Tenses can be simple or compound.

Simple tenses add endings to the stem of the verb:

present	lavor**o**	*I work/I am working*
future	lavor**erò**	*I will work*
imperfect	lavor**avo**	*I was working*
simple past	lavor**ai**	*I worked*

Compound tenses use a form of the verb called the past participle, together with **avere** or **essere** as an auxiliary (helping) verb:

| *perfect* | **ho** lavorato | *I have worked/I worked* |
| *pluperfect* | **avevo** lavorato | *I had worked* |

29.5 Regular and irregular verbs

Regular Italian verbs divide into three groups, according to the infinitive ending: -**are**, -**ere** or -**ire**. Each group follows a predictable pattern in each of the tenses (see 47).

Irregular verbs have forms which do not follow these patterns and must be learnt separately (see 48 and 49). Some verbs may be irregular in one tense only, others in several.

- -**are** verbs form the largest group of verbs. Most of them are regular:

abitare	*to live*	cambiare	*to change*
comprare	*to buy*	firmare	*to sign*
parlare	*to speak*	pensare	*to think*

There are only four irregular -**are** verbs:

andare	*to go*
dare	*to give*
fare	*to make*
stare	*to stay*

- Many -**ere** verbs are irregular, some in the past tenses only, others in all tenses.

- -**ire** verbs form the smallest group. In some tenses they subdivide into two groups (see 30.3).

■ **29.5.1** A few irregular verbs have infinitives ending in -**arre**, -**orre** and -**urre**. These follow the patterns shown in 48 for the following verbs:

trarre	*to pull*
porre	*to put*
produrre	*to produce*

The present tense

The present tense of regular verbs is formed by adding the endings shown in bold type to the stem of the verb. In the present tense, **-ire** verbs divide into two groups.

	-are	-ere	-ire (1)	-ire (2)
io	lavoro	vendo	parto	capisco
tu	lavori	vendi	parti	capisci
lui/lei/Lei	lavora	vende	parte	capisce
noi	lavoriamo	vendiamo	partiamo	capiamo
voi	lavorate	vendete	partite	capite
loro	lavorano	vendono	partono	capiscono

30.1 Spelling, pronunciation and stress

■ **30.1.1** In the **tu** and **noi** forms:

- most verbs ending in **-ciare** and **-giare** drop one **i**:

infinitive	tu	noi
cominciare	cominci	cominciamo
mangiare	mangi	mangiamo

- verbs ending in **-care** and **-gare** insert **h** before the endings:

giocare	giochi	giochiamo
spiegare	spieghi	spieghiamo

■ **30.1.2** In the **io** and **loro** forms, the pronunciation of **c** and **g** in verbs ending in **-cere, gere, -gire** changes:

infinitive	io	loro
vincere	vinco	vincono
leggere	leggo	leggono
fuggire	fuggo	fuggono

■ **30.1.3** In the **loro** form the stress is usually on the syllable before the **-ano/-ono** ending, never on the ending itself:

mangiano **par**tono co**min**ciano fi**nis**cono

30.2 Use of the present tense

The present tense is used to talk about an action which:

- is happening at the time of speaking:

Lavoro oggi.	*I am working today.*
Il treno arriva.	*The train is arriving.*

- happens repeatedly or is on-going:

Lavoro ogni giorno.	*I work every day.*
Alessandra parla francese.	*Alessandra speaks French.*

- started in the past and is still going on:

Lavoro da tre anni.	*I have been working for three years.*
Studiano l'italiano da settembre.	*They have been learning Italian since September.*

- is about to happen at a stated time in the future:

Lavoro domani.	*I am working tomorrow.*
Partiamo per l'Italia in aprile.	*We are leaving for Italy in April.*

■ **30.2.1** Unlike English, the present tense in Italian does not use auxiliary verbs, i.e. verbs which assist the main verb:

Lavoro.	*I am working.*
Lavora?	***Are** you working?* ***Do** you work?*
Luigi non lavora.	*Luigi is not working/**does** not work.*

30.3 -ire verbs

In the present tense, **-ire** verbs divide into two groups. One group inserts **-isc** before all endings except **noi** and **voi**.

There is no means of telling which group a verb belongs to – this has to be learnt. The following are examples of each type:

without -isc	*with -isc*
aprire *to open*	capire *to understand*
avvertire *to warn*	colpire *to hit*
bollire *to boil*	costruire *to build*
consentire *to consent*	distribuire *to distribute*
coprire *to cover*	finire *to finish*
divertire *to amuse*	fornire *to provide*
dormire *to sleep*	preferire *to prefer*
offrire *to offer*	proibire *to prohibit*
partire *to leave*	pulire *to clean*
seguire *to follow*	punire *to punish*
sentire *to hear/to feel*	spedire *to send*
servire *to serve*	suggerire *to suggest*
vestire *to dress*	unire *to unite*

A few **-ire** verbs can be used with or without **-isc**. The most common are:

applaudire *to applaud*	mentire *to lie*
inghiottire *to swallow*	tossire *to cough*

30.4 The present continuous

As an alternative to the present tense, **stare** can be used with the gerund (see 39) to express 'I am ...ing', 'you are ...ing', etc. However, it is not as widely used in Italian as in English, and is only used to emphasize that something is in progress at the very time of speaking.

Imparo l'italiano.	*I am learning Italian.*
Sto imparando i verbi ora.	*I am learning the verbs now.*
Lavora in ufficio.	*He works in the office.*
Sta lavorando in ufficio.	*He's working in the office.*

30.5 Irregular present tense forms

Many verbs are irregular in the present tense, including **essere** (*to be*), **avere** (*to have*) and **andare** (*to go*). The most commonly used are shown in 48 and 49.

31 The future tense

The future tense of regular verbs is formed by adding the endings shown in bold type to the stem of the verb.

	-are	-ere	-ire
io	lavor**erò**	vend**erò**	cap**irò**
tu	lavor**erai**	vend**erai**	cap**irai**
lui/lei/Lei	lavor**erà**	vend**erà**	cap**irà**
noi	lavor**eremo**	vend**eremo**	cap**iremo**
voi	lavor**erete**	vend**erete**	cap**irete**
loro	lavor**eranno**	vend**eranno**	cap**iranno**

31.1 Spelling

Some -**are** verbs change their spelling before all the future endings:

- verbs ending in -**ciare** and -**giare** drop the i:
  cominciare   comincerò, comincerai, etc.
  mangiare   mangerò, mangerai, etc.

- verbs ending in -**care** and -**gare** insert **h**:
  giocare   giocherò, giocherai, etc.
  pagare   pagherò, pagherai, etc.

31.2 Use of the future tense

The future corresponds to the English 'will/shall do'.
It is used:

- to talk about an action which will take place at a later date
  Ti telefonerò più tardi.   *I'll phone you later.*
  Partiranno fra poco.   *They will leave soon.*

- to express 'to be going to ...':

  Dormiranno qui.   { *They're going to sleep here.*
                       { *They'll sleep here.*

  Come pagherai?   { *How are you going to pay?*
                      { *How will you pay?*

- to express probability:

Dov'è Luca? Sarà in ufficio.   *Where's Luca? He'll be in the office.*

Marta avrà trent'anni.   *Marta is probably thirty.*

- after **se** (*if*), **quando** (*when*), **appena** (*as soon as*), **finché** (*until*), when the other verb in the sentence is in the future:

Se potrà venire, mi telefonerà?   *If you're able to come, will you phone me?*

Quando andrò in tabaccheria, comprerò dei francobolli.   *When I go to the tobacconist's, I'll buy some stamps.*

■ **31.2.1** The present tense, not the future, is used:

- in everyday speech, to talk about something arranged for the future:

Partiamo domani.   *We're leaving tomorrow.*

Vado in vacanza in giugno.   *I'm going on holiday in June.*

- in questions like the following, introduced by 'shall':

Ti aspetto?   *Shall I wait for you?*

Paghiamo noi?   *Shall we pay?*

31.3 Irregular future tense forms

In the future tense, with the exception of **essere**, irregular verbs differ only slightly from the regular patterns.

■ **31.3.1**

essere *to be*   sarò, sarai, sarà, saremo, sarete, saranno

■ **31.3.2**

dare *to give*   darò, darai, darà, daremo, darete, daranno

fare *to do*   farò, farai, farà, faremo, farete, faranno

stare *to stay/to be*   starò, starai, starà, staremo, starete, staranno

■ **31.3.3** The following drop the first vowel of the ending:

andare to go	andrò, andrai, andrà, andremo, andrete, andranno
avere to have	avrò, avrai, avrà, avremo, avrete, avranno
cadere to fall	cadrò, cadrai, cadrà, cadremo, cadrete, cadranno
dovere to have to	dovrò, dovrai, dovrà, dovremo, dovrete, dovranno
potere to be able to	potrò, potrai, potrà, potremo, potrete, potranno
sapere to know	saprò, saprai, saprà, sapremo, saprete, sapranno
vedere to see	vedrò, vedrai, vedrà, vedremo, vedrete, vedranno
vivere to live	vivrò, vivrai, vivrà, vivremo, vivrete, vivranno

■ **31.3.4** A few verbs end in **-rro**, **-rrai**, etc., including:

bere to drink	berrò, berrai, berrà, berremo, berrete, berranno
porre to put	porrò, porrai, porrà, porremo, porrete, porranno
rimanere to stay	rimarrò, rimarrai, rimarrà, rimarremo, rimarrete, rimarranno
tenere to hold	terrò, terrai, terrà, terremo, terrete, terranno
venire to come	verrò, verrai, verrà, verremo, verrete, verranno
volere to want	vorrò, vorrai, vorrà, vorremo, vorrete, vorranno

31.4 Similarities in form between the future and the conditional

The future and conditional share certain characteristics:

• they incur the same spelling changes:

infinitive	future	conditional
comin**ciare**	comin**cerò**	comin**cerei**
pa**gare**	pa**gherò**	pa**gherei**

• verbs which have irregular future forms (see 31.3) are also irregular in the conditional, for example:

infinitive	future	conditional
essere	sarò	sarei
dare	darò	darei
andare	andrò	andrei
bere	berrò	berrei

The conditional

32

The conditional of regular verbs is formed by adding the endings shown in bold type to the stem of the verb.

	-are	**-ere**	**-ire**
io	lavor**erei**	vend**erei**	cap**irei**
tu	lavor**eresti**	vend**eresti**	cap**iresti**
lui/lei/Lei	lavor**erebbe**	vend**erebbe**	cap**irebbe**
noi	lavor**eremmo**	vend**eremmo**	cap**iremmo**
voi	lavor**ereste**	vend**ereste**	cap**ireste**
loro	lavor**erebbero**	vend**erebbero**	cap**irebbero**

32.1 Use of the conditional

The conditional is used:

- to express the English 'would do' (except as used in 33.1):
  Lavorerei domani, ma devo   *I would work tomorrow, but*
  andare dal dentista.   *I have to go to the dentist's.*
  Preferiresti andare ad   *Would you prefer to go to*
  Orvieto?   *Orvieto?*

- to express polite wishes or requests:
  Vorrei andare.   *I would like to go.*
  Mi darebbe l'indirizzo?   *Would you give me the address?*

- to convey that what is being said is only an opinion. It corresponds to the English 'it is alleged that', and similar expressions, in press reports:
  La vittima sarebbe morta   *It is believed that the victim*
  prima delle sette.   *died before seven o'clock.*

■ **32.1.1** When a verb in the conditional is linked to 'if' + another verb, the verb in the 'if' part of the sentence is in the imperfect subjunctive (see 42.2, 42.7.3):

Lavorerei domani se non   *I would work tomorrow if I*
dovessi andare dal dentista.   *didn't have to go to the dentist's.*
Ci andrei se avessi tempo.   *I would go if I had time.*

33 The imperfect tense

The imperfect tense of regular verbs is formed by adding the endings shown in bold type to the stem of the verb.

	-are	-ere	-ire
io	lavor**avo**	vend**evo**	cap**ivo**
tu	lavor**avi**	vend**evi**	cap**ivi**
lui/lei/Lei	lavor**ava**	vend**eva**	cap**iva**
noi	lavor**avamo**	vend**evamo**	cap**ivamo**
voi	lavor**avate**	vend**evate**	cap**ivate**
loro	lavor**avano**	vend**evano**	cap**ivano**

33.1 Use of the imperfect tense

The imperfect is a past tense, used:

- to say that something continued over a period of time:

  Nel 1976 lavoravo a Londra. — *In 1976 I was working/worked in London.*

  Con chi parlava? — *Who were you talking to?*

  Sperava di venire. — *She was hoping/hoped to come.*

- to talk about things which used to happen repeatedly:

  Andavamo al mare d'estate. — *In the summer, we used to go/went to the seaside.*

  Ogni giorno ci alzavamo tardi. — *Every day we would get up late/ got up late.*

- in descriptions:

  Quando avevo vent'anni ... — *When I was twenty ...*

  Erano felici. — *They were happy.*

- to say that something was going on when something else happened:

  Aspettavo l'autobus quando ho visto un incidente. — *I was waiting for the bus when I saw an accident.*

  Mentre mangiavamo, mia zia ha telefonato. — *While we were eating, my aunt phoned.*

- to say something had been going on FOR some time or SINCE a particular time:

  Lavoravo **da** due mesi. *I'd been working for two months.*

  Aspettavamo **da** domenica. *We'd been waiting since Sunday.*

33.2 The imperfect continuous

The imperfect of **stare** can be used with the gerund (see 39) to emphasize that something was in progress when something else happened.

Stavo leggendo quando ho sentito un rumore. *I was reading when I heard a noise.*

33.3 Irregular imperfect tense forms

Only a few verbs are irregular in the imperfect:

■ 33.3.1

essere *to be* ero, eri, era, eravamo, eravate, erano

■ 33.3.2 The following verbs have irregular stems to which regular **-ere** endings are added:

bere *to drink* bevevo, bevevi, beveva, bevevamo, bevevate, bevevano
dire *to day* dicevo, dicevi, diceva, dicevamo, dicevate, dicevano
fare *to make* facevo, facevi, faceva, facevamo, facevate, facevano
trarre *to pull* traevo, traevi, traeva, traevamo, traevate, traevano
porre *to put* ponevo, ponevi, poneva, ponevamo, ponevate,ponevano
produrre producevo, producevi, produceva, producevamo,
to produce producevate, producevano

... and verbs which end in **-dire**, **-fare**, **-arre**, **-orre** and **-urre**.

34 The simple past tense

The simple past tense is known in Italian as the **passato remoto**; it has various English names, including past definite, preterite and past historic.

The simple past of regular verbs is formed by adding the endings shown in bold type to the stem of the verb.

There are alternative forms for the **io**, **lui/lei/Lei** and **loro** forms of -**ere** verbs.

	-are	-ere	-ire
io	lavorai	vendei/-etti	capii
tu	lavorasti	vendesti	capisti
lui/lei/Lei	lavorò	vendé/-ette	capì
noi	lavorammo	vendemmo	capimmo
voi	lavoraste	vendeste	capiste
loro	lavorarono	venderono/-ettero	capirono

34.1 Use of the simple past tense

- The simple past is used to say that something took place, and was completed, in the past.

  Nel 1940 lo scrittore tornò in Sicilia.   *In 1940 the writer returned to Sicily.*

  Morì dieci anni dopo.   *He died ten years later.*

  Ascoltarono in silenzio, poi partirono.   *They listened in silence, then they left.*

- Its use is restricted to:
  - formal writing
  - formal speech
  - everyday speech in some parts of Tuscany and Southern Italy.

In most cases, the tense used to refer to past events is the perfect tense (see 35):

Anna è tornata ieri.   *Anna came back yesterday.*

Hanno ascoltato.   *They listened.*

34.2 Irregular simple past forms

Most common irregular verbs like **avere**, **dire**, **essere**, **fare**, **venire**, are irregular in the simple past (see 48).
Many **-ere** verbs are irregular in the simple past only.

■ **34.2.1** Verbs ending in -dere, -ndere and -gere:
-dere e.g. **chiedere** to ask, **chiudere** to close, **decidere** to decide, **dividere** to divide, **offendere** to offend, **perdere** to lose
chiedere chiesi, chiedesti, chiese, chiedemmo, chiedeste, chie**sero**

-ndere e.g. **dipendere** to depend, **nascondere** to hide, **prendere** to take **rispondere** to reply, **scendere** to go down, **spendere** to spend
dipendere dipesi, dipendesti, dipese, dipendemmo, dipendeste, dipe**sero**

-gere e.g. **accorgersi** to realise, **dipingere** to paint, **fingere** to pretend **giungere** to reach, **piangere** to cry, **volgere** to turn
accorgersi mi accorsi, ti accorgesti, si accorse, ci accorgemmo, vi accorgeste, si accor**sero**

■ **34.2.2** Other verbs with irregular simple past forms:

cadere to fall	caddi, cadesti, cadde, cademmo, cadeste, caddero
conoscere to know	conobbi, conoscesti, conobbe, conoscemmo, conosceste, conobbero
correre to run	corsi, corresti, corse, corremmo, correste, corsero
crescere to grow	crebbi, crescesti, crebbe, crescemmo, cresceste, crebbero
dirigere to direct	diressi, dirigesti, diresse, dirigemmo, dirigeste, diressero
discutere to discuss	discussi, discutesti, discusse, discutemmo, discuteste, discussero
leggere to read	lessi, leggesti, lesse, leggemmo, leggeste, lessero
mettere to put	misi, mettesti, mise, mettemmo, metteste, misero
nascere to be born	nacqui, nascesti, nacque, nascemmo, nasceste, nacquero
rompere to break	ruppi, rompesti, ruppe, rompemmo, rompeste, ruppero
scrivere to write	scrissi, scrivesti, scrisse, scrivemmo, scriveste, scrissero
vedere to see	vidi, vedesti, vide, vedemmo, vedeste, videro
vincere to win	vinsi, vincesti, vinse, vincemmo, vinceste, vinsero
vivere to live	vissi, vivesti, visse, vivemmo, viveste, vissero

35 The perfect tense

The perfect tense is a past tense known in Italian as the **passato prossimo**. It is formed from the present tense of **avere** or **essere** (the auxiliary verbs) plus the past participle of the main verb.

35.1 Past participle

The past participle of regular verbs is formed by replacing the infinitive ending as follows:

-are → -ato	lavor**are** *to work*	→ lavor**ato** *worked*
-ere → -uto	vend**ere** *to sell*	→ vend**uto** *sold*
-ire → -ito	part**ire** *to leave*	→ part**ito** *left*

Some verbs ending in **-cere** add **i** before **-uto**:

conosc**ere** *to know*	→ conosc**iuto** *known*
piac**ere** *to please*	→ piac**iuto** *pleased*

35.2 Perfect tense with avere

	-are	-ere	-ire
io	ho lavorato	ho venduto	ho capito
tu	hai lavorato	hai venduto	hai capito
lui/lei/Lei	ha lavorato	ha venduto	ha capito
noi	abbiamo lavorato	abbiamo venduto	abbiamo capito
voi	avete lavorato	avete venduto	avete capito
loro	hanno lavorato	hanno venduto	hanno capito

35.3 Perfect tense with essere

	-are	-ere	-ire
io	sono andato/a	sono caduto/a	sono partito/a
tu	sei andato/a	sei caduto/a	sei partito/a
lui/lei/Lei	è andato/a	è caduto/a	è partito/a
noi	siamo andati/e	siamo caduti/e	siamo partiti/e
voi	siete andati/e	siete caduti/e	siete partiti/e
loro	sono andati/e	sono caduti/e	sono partiti/e

35.4 Use of the perfect tense

The perfect tense corresponds to more than one English past tense – **ho mangiato** is 'I ate' and 'I have eaten'. In spoken Italian it is used far more than the simple past (34).

Hanno scritto al direttore.	*{They wrote to the manager.* *{They have written to the manager.*
Hanno scritto al direttore?	*{Did they write to the manager?* *{Have they written to the manager?*

Il treno è partito.	*The train has left.*
Il treno è partito alle due.	*The train left at two o'clock.*
Il treno è partito alle due?	*Did the train leave at two o'clock?*

35.5 avere or essere?

■ **35.5.1** Most verbs form the perfect tense with **avere**.

■ **35.5.2** Verbs forming the perfect tense with **essere** include:

- verbs relating to existence:

essere *to be*	**stare** *to be/to stay*
nascere *to be born*	**morire** *to die*
esistere *to exist*	**valere** *to be worth*
divenire *to become*	**diventare** *to become*

- many verbs of movement, and related verbs:

andare *to go*	**venire** *to come*
arrivare *to arrive*	**partire** *to leave*
entrare *to enter*	**restare/rimanere** *to stay*
apparire *to appear*	**sparire** *to disappear*
cadere *to fall*	**scadere** *to run out/to expire*
tornare *to return*	**ritornare** *to return*
uscire *to go out*	**riuscire** *to succeed/to manage*

- impersonal verbs (see 45)

Ci è voluto molto tempo.	*It took a lot of time.*
Che cosa è successo?	*What's happened?*

- reflexive verbs (see 43)

Ti sei divertito?	*Have you enjoyed yourself?*
Si sono sposati nel 1994.	*They got married in 1994.*

■ **35.5.3** The modal verbs **dovere**, **potere** and **volere** (see 44) take **avere** or **essere** in the perfect tense, according to which one the verb that follows would normally take:

Ho dovuto aspettare.	*I had to wait.*
Sono dovuto partire.	*I had to leave.*
Non ha potuto prenotare.	*He couldn't book.*
Non è potuto uscire.	*He couldn't go out.*

The tendency in speech is to use **avere** with all verbs:

Ho dovuto partire.	Non ha potuto uscire.

■ **35.5.4** Some verbs which normally take **avere** can take **essere** when they are used without a direct object:

cominciare *to start*	**finire** *to finish*
aumentare *to increase*	**diminuire** *to decrease*
cambiare *to change*	**crescere** *to grow*
Ho finito questo libro.	*I have finished this book.*
Il programma è finito.	*The programme has finished.*

A few **essere** verbs take **avere** when there is a direct object:

salire *to go up*	**scendere** *to go down*
È salito in macchina	*He got into the car.*
Ha salito le scale.	*He went upstairs.*

35.6 Agreement

■ **35.6.1** The past participle of a verb taking **essere** agrees with the subject of the verb:

Il signor Rossi è arrivato.	*Mr Rossi has arrived.*
La signora Rossi è arrivata.	*Mrs Rossi has arrived.*
Il signor Rossi e sua figlia sono arrivati.	*Mr Rossi and his daughter have arrived.*
Le due figlie sono arrivate.	*The two girls have arrived.*

■ **35.6.2** The past participle of a verb taking **avere** does not normally change. However, if there is a direct object pronoun (**lo**, **la**, **li** or **le**), the past participle agrees with the pronoun. **Lo** and **la** are generally shortened to **l'**.

Giorgio? L'ho visto oggi.	*Giorgio? I saw him today.*
Anna? L'ho vista oggi.	*Anna? I saw her today.*
Giorgio e Anna? Li ho visti oggi.	*Giorgio and Anna? I saw them today.*
Maria e Anna? Le ho viste oggi.	*Maria and Anna? I saw them today.*

35.7 Negatives with the perfect tense

The negative **non** is placed before **avere** or **essere**:

Non ho pagato.	*I haven't paid.*
Non siamo andati.	*We didn't go.*

Some negative words go between **avere/essere** and the past participle (see 17.3):

Non ho ancora pagato.	*I haven't paid yet.*
Non ci sono mai stato.	*I've never been there.*

Others go after the past participle (see 17.2):

Non hanno incontrato nessuno.	*They didn't meet anybody.*
Non ho comprato niente.	*I've bought nothing.*

35.8 Pronouns with the perfect tense

Pronouns go before **avere/essere**:

Mi hanno invitato a cena.	*They invited me to dinner.*
Me l'hanno già detto.	*They have already told me.*
Gliel'ho dato.	*I have given it to you.*
Vi ha scritto due volte.	*He has written to you twice.*

Ci and **ne** follow the same rules:

Ci sono andato ieri.	*I went there yesterday.*
Ne ho comprati due.	*I bought two.*

36 Other compound tenses

As well as the perfect tense, several other tenses are formed using **avere** and **essere** and the past participle. In these tenses, the use of **avere** or **essere** is the same as for the perfect tense (see 35.5). Agreement, negatives and the position of pronouns are also the same (see 35.6–35.8).

36.1 The pluperfect

The pluperfect is formed from the imperfect of **avere** or **essere** and the past participle:

	with *avere*	with *essere*
io	avevo lavorato	ero partito/a
tu	avevi lavorato	eri partito/a
lui/lei/Lei	aveva lavorato	era partito/a
noi	avevamo lavorato	eravamo partiti/e
voi	avevate lavorato	eravate partiti/e
loro	avevano lavorato	erano partiti/e

■ **36.1.1** The pluperfect corresponds to the English 'had done':

Avevo prenotato i posti.	*I had booked seats.*
Avevate già visto il film?	*Had you already seen the film?*
Eri già partito quando io sono arrivato.	*You had already left when I arrived.*
Non eravamo ancora entrati.	*We had not yet gone in.*

36.2 The future perfect

The future perfect is formed from the future tense of **avere** or **essere** and the past participle:

	with *avere*	with *essere*
io	avrò lavorato	sarò partito/a
tu	avrai lavorato	sarai partito/a
lui/lei/Lei	avrà lavorato	sarà partito/a
noi	avremo lavorato	saremo partiti/e
voi	avrete lavorato	sarete partiti/e
loro	avranno lavorato	saranno partiti/e

■ **36.2.1** The future perfect tense corresponds to the English 'will have done'. It is used:

- to say what will have happened by a particular time:

  Il treno sarà arrivato prima delle cinque.
  The train will have arrived before five o'clock.

  Avrà ricevuto la lettera entro il 25.
  She will have received the letter by the 25th.

- to suggest that something has probably happened:

  Avrà visto tutto ormai.
  He will have seen everything by now.

  Sarà arrivato verso le otto.
  He will have arrived at about eight o'clock./He probably arrived at about eight o'clock.

- after **se** (*if*), **quando** (*when*), **appena** (*as soon as*), **finché** (*until*), **fino a quando** (*until*), when the main verb of the sentence is in the future. In English, the perfect tense, or even the present, is used instead.

  Quando avrò finito, uscirò.
  When I've finished, I'll go out.

  Aspetteremo fino a quando Roberto sarà tornato.
  We'll wait until Roberto comes back.

36.3 The past conditional

The past conditional is formed from the simple conditional of **avere** or **essere** and the past participle.

	with avere	*with essere*
io	avrei lavorato	sarei partito/a
tu	avresti lavorato	saresti partito/a
lui/lei/Lei	avrebbe lavorato	sarebbe partito/a
noi	avremmo lavorato	saremmo partiti/e
voi	avreste lavorato	sareste partiti/e
loro	avrebbero lavorato	sarebbero partiti/e

■ **36.3.1** The past conditional corresponds to the English 'would have done'. It is used:

- to say what would have happened:

| Sarei rimasto, ma ero molto stanco. | *I would have stayed, but I was very tired.* |
| Avremmo preferito un vino secco. | *We would have preferred a dry wine.* |

It is often linked to 'if' + pluperfect subjunctive (see 42.4, 42.7.3).

| Sarei rimasto se non avessi già speso tutti i soldi. | *I would have stayed if I hadn't already spent all my money.* |
| Avrebbe risposto se avesse ricevuto il messaggio. | *He would have replied if he had received the message.* |

- in indirect constructions, when the main verb of a sentence is in the past tense. The simple conditional is used in English:

| Ha detto che sarebbe venuta. | *She said she would come.* |
| Pensavo che avrebbe telefonato. | *I thought he would phone.* |

36.4 The past anterior

The past anterior is formed from the simple past of **avere** or **essere** and the past participle.

	with *avere*	with *essere*
io	ebbi lavorato	fui partito/a
tu	avesti lavorato	fosti partito/a
lui/lei/Lei	ebbe lavorato	fu partito/a
noi	avemmo lavorato	fummo partiti/e
voi	aveste lavorato	foste partiti/e
loro	ebbero lavorato	furono partiti/e

■ **36.4.1** The past anterior is translated into English by 'had done'. It is only used with the simple past (see 34), and its use is usually restricted to formal writing and formal speech.

Quando ebbero firmato il documento, partirono.

When they had signed the document, they left.

37 The passive

When something is done TO the subject, not BY the subject, the verb is said to be in the passive voice. The passive is formed in Italian from **essere** or **venire** and the past participle, which agrees with the subject. The passive can also be formed with **andare**, but this has a slightly different meaning.

(Another way to express the passive is to use **si** – see 22.)

37.1 essere

The past participle can be used with all tenses of **essere**:

Il vino bianco è servito fresco.	White wine is served chilled.
La torta è stata fatta in casa.	The cake was made at home.
Le fragole saranno servite con panna.	The strawberries will be served with cream.
I ravioli erano stati fatti il giorno prima.	The ravioli had been made the day before.

37.2 venire

The simple tenses of **venire** can be used instead of **essere**:

Il vino bianco viene servito fresco.	White wine is served chilled.
La pasta veniva fatta in casa.	The pasta used to be made at home.
I vini verranno imbottigliati fra poco.	The wines will be bottled soon.

37.3 andare

The present tense of **andare** is used to say that something must/should be done:

Il vino bianco va servito fresco.	White wine should be served chilled.
Le tagliatelle vanno cotte a parte.	The tagliatelle must be cooked separately.

The past participle is the form of the verb which follows **avere** and **essere** in compound tenses (see 35, 36), and which is used in passive constructions (see 37).

The past participle of regular verbs is formed by changing the infinitive endings as follows:

-are → -ato	lavor**are** *to work*	→ lavor**ato** *worked*
-ere → -uto	vend**ere** *to sell*	→ vend**uto** *sold*
-ire → -ito	part**ire** *to leave*	→ part**ito** *left*

38.1 The past participle as an adjective

The past participle of some verbs can be used as adjectives:

Questo è il mio vino **preferito**.	*This is my favourite wine.*
È così **pulita** la camera.	*The room is so clean.*

38.2 having ...

The past participle can be used alone where English would use 'having done' or a phrase beginning 'when ...':

Perduto l'indirizzo, ho dovuto telefonare in ufficio.	*Having lost the address, I had to phone the office.*
Tornato a casa, ho trovato il messaggio.	*When I returned/Having returned home, I found the message.*

38.3 appena/non appena

Appena or **non appena** followed by the past participle correspond to 'as soon as ...':

(Non) appena tornato a casa, ho trovato il messaggio.	*As soon as I returned home, I found the message.*
(Non) appena arrivati, siamo andati alla spiaggia.	*As soon as we arrived, we went to the beach.*

38.4 Irregular past participles

■ **38.4.1** **Fare** is the only -**are** verb with an irregular past participle: **fatto**.

■ **38.4.2** Many -**ere** verbs have irregular past participles. Examples from the main groups are given below.

-dere and **-ndere → -so**

chiudere	*to close*	chiuso
decidere	*to decide*	deciso
offendere	*to offend*	offeso
prendere	*to take*	preso
scendere	*to go down*	sceso
spendere	*to spend*	speso
uccidere	*to kill*	ucciso

... except

chiedere	*to ask*	chiesto
nascondere	*to hide*	nascosto
rispondere	*to reply*	risposto
succedere	*to happen*	successo
vedere	*to see*	visto/veduto

-gere → -to and **-ggere → -tto**

accorgersi	*to realize*	accorto
aggiungere	*to add*	aggiunto
dipingere	*to paint*	dipinto
friggere	*to fry*	fritto
leggere	*to read*	letto
piangere	*to cry*	pianto
proteggere	*to protect*	protetto
volgere	*to turn*	volto

... except

dirigere	*to direct*	diretto
stringere	*to squeeze*	stretto

-gliere → -lto

accogliere	*to welcome*	accolto
scegliere	*to choose*	scelto
togliere	*to take off*	tolto

38.4.3 Other -ere verbs with irregular past participles:

bere	*to drink*	bevuto
correre	*to run*	corso
discutere	*to discuss*	discusso
essere	*to be*	stato
mettere	*to put*	messo
muovere	*to move*	mosso
nascere	*to be born*	nato
rimanere	*to stay*	rimasto
rompere	*to break*	rotto
scrivere	*to write*	scritto
vincere	*to win*	vinto
vivere	*to live*	vissuto

38.4.4 Irregular past participles of -ire verbs include:

apparire	*to appear*	apparso
aprire	*to open*	aperto
coprire	*to cover*	coperto
dire	*to say*	detto
morire	*to die*	morto
offrire	*to offer*	offerto
soffrire	*to suffer*	sofferto
venire	*to come*	venuto

38.4.5 Verbs ending in -arre, -orre and -urre form the past participle as follows:

trarre	*to pull*	tratto
porre	*to put*	posto
produrre	*to produce*	prodotto

The gerund is the form of the verb which ends in '-ing' in English. The gerund of regular verbs is formed by changing the infinitive endings as follows:

-are → -ando	lavor**are** *to work*	→	lavor**ando** *working*
-ere → -endo	vend**ere** *to sell*	→	vend**endo** *selling*
-ire → -endo	part**ire** *to leave*	→	part**endo** *leaving*

39.1 Use of the gerund

The gerund is used:

- to say 'by', 'on' or 'while' doing:

Vedendoli, ha sorriso.	*On seeing them, she smiled.*
Leggendo il giornale, ho visto il suo nome.	*While reading the paper, I saw his name.*
L'abbiamo fatto seguendo il loro esempio.	*We did it by following their example.*

- with the present tense of **stare** to say that something is in progress at the moment (present continuous, see 30.4):

Che cosa sta facendo?	*What are you doing?*
Non posso venire, sto guardando la partita.	*I can't come, I'm watching the match.*

- with the imperfect of **stare** to say what was happening at the time when something else happened (imperfect continuous, see 33.2):

Stavo lavorando quando Stefano ha telefonato.	*I was working when Stefano rang.*
Stavano entrando quando io sono arrivata.	*They were just going in when I arrived.*

- with **pur**, a shortened form of **pure**, to mean 'even though':

Pur avendo una mappa, non ho trovato il paesino.	*Even though I had a map, I didn't find the village.*

■ **39.1.1** The use of the gerund is not as common in Italian as in English. The present tense or imperfect tense is used far more often than **stare** + gerund.

Also, it is incorrect to use the Italian gerund after **prima di** (*before*), **invece di** (*instead*), **oltre a** (*as well as*), **senza** (*without*) (see 40.2.2), or **dopo** (*after*) (see 40.5.1):

prima di uscire	*before going out*
senza parlare	*without speaking*

39.2 Pronouns with the gerund

Pronouns follow the gerund and combine with it to form one word (see 20.6.2):

Parland**ogli**, ho imparato che ...	*Talking to him, I learnt that ...*
Guardand**olo**, ho visto ...	*Looking at him, I saw ...*

... except when the gerund is used with **stare**:

Gli stavo parlando quando ...	*I was talking to him when ...*
Lo sto guardando.	*I'm watching him.*

39.3 Irregular gerunds

Most verbs, including **essere** and **avere**, have regular gerund forms, but a few form the gerund by adding **-endo** to irregular stems:

bere	*to drink*	**bev**endo
dire	*to say*	**dic**endo
fare	*to make*	**fac**endo
trarre	*to pull*	**tra**endo
porre	*to put*	**pon**endo
produrre	*to produce*	**produc**endo

Other verbs ending in **-dire**, **-fare**, **-arre**, **-orre** and **-urre** follow the same patterns.

40 The infinitive

The infinitive of a verb is the basic form found in the dictionary. In Italian, the infinitive of nearly all verbs ends in **-are**, **-ere** or **-ire**.

The infinitive is used in Italian after other verbs, after prepositions, as a noun, and to give instructions. The English equivalent often starts with 'to ...' or ends in '-ing'.

40.1 The infinitive after other verbs

■ **40.1.1** When one verb follows another, the second is in the infinitive (except in the compound tenses where the first verb is **avere** or **essere** and the second is a past participle):

Vorrei telefonare in Inghilterra.	*I'd like to phone England.*
Mi può aiutare?	*Can you help me?*
Deve fare il numero.	*You have to dial the number.*
Bisogna sapere il prefisso.	*You have to know the code.*
Basta aspettare.	*All you have to do is wait.*
L'ho sentito parlare.	*I heard him talking.*
Le dispiace ripetere?	*Would you mind repeating?*

■ **40.1.2** Impersonal expressions with **essere** + adjective also follow this pattern (see 45.5):

È inutile lamentarsi.	*It's no use complaining.*

40.2 The infinitive after prepositions

■ **40.2.1** The infinitive often follows a preposition.

Comincio a capire.	*I'm beginning to understand.*
Stai attento a non perderti.	*Mind you don't get lost.*
Sono curioso di sapere di dove sei.	*I'm curious to know where you are from.*
Speriamo di ritornare qui.	*We hope to come back here.*
Sei pronto per uscire?	*Are you ready to go out?*

■ **40.2.2** The infinitive is also used after **prima di** (*before*), **invece di** (*instead*), **oltre a** (*as well as*) and **senza** (*without*). The English translation ends in '-ing':

Hai chiuso la finestra prima di partire?	*Did you shut the window before leaving?*
Invece di tornare a casa, andiamo al cinema.	*Instead of going home, let's go to the cinema.*
Oltre a essere stanco, ho la nausea.	*As well as being tired, I feel sick.*
È partito senza rispondere.	*He left without answering.*

40.3 The infinitive as a noun

The infinitive (with **il/l'/lo** in more formal Italian) can be used as a noun:

Nuotare mi piace.	*I like swimming.*
Sciare non è molto facile.	*Skiing is not very easy.*
Lo scrivere è un'attività complessa.	*Writing is a complex activity.*

40.4 Giving instructions

The infinitive can be used to give official instructions or procedures in recipe books, manuals, etc.

Allacciare le cinture di sicurezza.	*Fasten your safety belts.*
Spingere. Tirare.	*Push. Pull.*
Non parlare al conducente.	*Please do not speak to the driver.*
Tagliare le verdure, tritare le cipolle e l'aglio.	*Cut the vegetables, chop the onions and garlic.*

40.5 The past infinitive

The infinitives **avere** and **essere**, followed by the past participle, correspond to the English 'to have done'. The final e of **avere** (and sometimes **essere**) is often dropped.

Sono fortunata di aver trovato questo posto.	*I'm lucky to have found this place.*
Che sollievo essere arrivato.	*What a relief to have arrived.*

■ **40.5.1** The past infinitive is used after **dopo** (*after*) and **ringraziare di/per** (*to thank for*):

Dopo aver mangiato siamo andati al cinema.	*After eating (i.e. after having eaten), we went to the cinema.*
Mezz'ora dopo essere arrivato, sono dovuto ripartire.	*Half an hour after arriving, I had to leave again.*
La ringrazio di aver scritto.	*Thank you for writing.*
Vi ringrazio per essere venuti.	*Thank you for coming.*

40.6 Irregular infinitives

Some verbs have infinitives ending in **-arre**, **-orre** or **-urre**:

-arre	trarre *to draw/to pull*	attrarre *to attract*
	contrarre *to contract*	distrarre *to distract*
	sottrarre *to subtract*	estrarre *to extract*
-orre	porre *to put*	comporre *to compose*
	disporre *to dispose*	esporre *to expose*
	imporre *to impose*	opporre *to oppose*
	proporre *to propose*	supporre *to suppose*
-urre	dedurre *to deduce*	introdurre *to introduce*
	produrre *to produce*	ridurre *to reduce*
	sedurre *to seduce*	tradurre *to translate*

1 The imperative

The imperative is used for giving instructions, directions and commands. The four commonly used imperative forms are **tu**, **Lei**, **noi** and **voi**. They are formed by adding the endings shown in bold type to the stem of the verb.

The **-ire** verbs divide into two groups as for the present tense (see 30.3).

	-are	-ere	-ire (1)	-ire (2)
tu	lavor**a**	vend**i**	part**i**	cap**isci**
Lei	lavor**i**	vend**a**	part**a**	cap**isca**
noi	lavor**iamo**	vend**iamo**	part**iamo**	cap**iamo**
voi	lavor**ate**	vend**ete**	part**ite**	cap**ite**

The **Lei** imperative is identical to the **Lei** form of the present subjunctive (see 42.1).

The **noi** and **voi** imperatives are identical to the **noi** and **voi** forms of the present tense (see 30).

A **loro** imperative exists, but is rarely used – the **voi** form is used instead.

41.1 Use of the imperative

The imperative is used:

- in the **tu**, **Lei** and **voi** forms, to give instructions to other people:

tu	Guida con cautela.	*Drive carefully.*
Lei	Giri a destra.	*Turn right.*
voi	Parlate piano, per favore.	*Talk quietly, please.*

- in the **noi** form, to make suggestions:

Andiamo.	*Let's go.*
Mangiamo subito.	*Let's eat straightaway.*

41.2 Negative imperatives

■ **41.2.1** The negative of the **Lei**, **noi** and **voi** imperative is formed by placing **non** before the affirmative imperative

Lei	Non prenda quella strada.	*Don't take that road.*
noi	Non rimaniamo qui.	*Let's not stay here.*
voi	Non dimenticate!	*Don't forget!*

■ **41.2.2** The negative of the **tu** imperative is formed by using **non** with the INFINITIVE of the verb.

Non guardare indietro.	*Don't look back.*
Non essere stupido.	*Don't be stupid.*

41.3 Irregular imperatives

■ **41.3.1** The following verbs have irregular **tu** imperatives:

andare	*to go*	**vai** *or* **va'**
avere	*to have*	**abbi**
dare	*to give*	**dai** *or* **da'**
dire	*to say*	**di'**
essere	*to be*	**sii**
fare	*to make*	**fai** *or* **fa'**
sapere	*to know*	**sappi**
stare	*to be, to stay*	**stai** *or* **sta'**

■ **41.3.2** Most verbs which are irregular in the present tense form the **Lei** imperative by changing the 1st person singular present tense ending from **-o** to **-a**:

infinitive		*io present*	*Lei imperative*
andare	*to go*	vado	**vada**
dire	*to say*	dico	**dica**
fare	*to make*	faccio	**faccia**
porre	*to put*	pongo	**ponga**
venire	*to come*	vengo	**venga**

■ **41.3.3** There are no irregular **noi** imperatives, and only **avere**, **essere** and **sapere** have irregular **voi** imperatives:

avere	to have	**abbiate**
essere	to be	**siate**
sapere	to know	**sappiate**

41.4 Pronouns with the imperative

Object pronouns, reflexive pronouns, **ci** (*there*) and **ne** all behave in the same way with the imperative.

■ **41.4.1** They go before the **Lei** imperative:

Mi scusi.	*Excuse me.*
Non **si** preoccupi.	*Don't worry.*
Ci vada domani.	*Go there tomorrow.*

■ **41.4.2** They go after all the other forms of the imperative, and combine with them to form one word:

tu	Scusa**mi**.	*Excuse me.*
	Ferma**ti**!	*Stop!*
	Non tocca**rlo**!	*Don't touch it!*
	Non preoccupa**rti**.	*Don't worry.*
noi	Andiamo**ci** domani.	*Let's go there tomorrow.*
	Compriamo**ne**.	*Let's buy some.*
	Non preoccupiamo**ci**.	*Let's not worry.*
voi	Mandate**melo**.	*Send it to me.*
	Non preoccupate**vi**.	*Don't worry.*

■ **41.4.3** The initial letter of a pronoun is doubled after the **tu** imperative of **andare**, **dare**, **dire** and **fare**:

Va**tt**ene!	*Go away!*
Da**mm**i la piantina.	*Give me the map.*
Di**mm**i la verità.	*Tell me the truth.*

... but **gli** does not change:

Da**gli** la piantina.	*Give him the map.*

42 The subjunctive

The subjunctive is used extensively in Italian to indicate uncertainty, possibility or personal attitudes rather than hard fact. There are four tenses of the subjunctive – present, imperfect, perfect and pluperfect.

42.1 Present subjunctive

The present subjunctive of nearly all verbs is formed by removing the -o from the **io** form of the present tense:

capire	capisco	capisc–
andare	vado	vad–
fare	faccio	facci–

... and adding the endings shown in bold type:

	-**are**	-**ere**	-**ire** (1)	-**ire** (2)
io	lavor**i**	vend**a**	part**a**	capisc**a**
tu	lavor**i**	vend**a**	part**a**	capisc**a**
lui/lei/Lei	lavor**i**	vend**a**	part**a**	capisc**a**
noi	lavor**iamo**	vend**iamo**	part**iamo**	cap**iamo**
voi	lavor**iate**	vend**iate**	part**iate**	cap**iate**
loro	lavor**ino**	vend**ano**	part**ano**	capisc**ano**

42.2 Imperfect subjunctive

The imperfect subjunctive is formed by adding the endings shown in bold type to the verb stem.

	-**are**	-**ere**	-**ire**
io	lavor**assi**	vend**essi**	cap**issi**
tu	lavor**assi**	vend**essi**	cap**issi**
lui/lei/Lei	lavor**asse**	vend**esse**	cap**isse**
noi	lavor**assimo**	vend**essimo**	cap**issimo**
voi	lavor**aste**	vend**este**	cap**iste**
loro	lavor**assero**	vend**essero**	cap**issero**

42.3 Perfect subjunctive

The perfect subjunctive is formed with the present subjunctive of **avere** or **essere** and the past participle:

	with **avere**	with **essere**
io	abbia lavorato	sia arrivato/a
tu	abbia lavorato	sia arrivato/a
lui/lei/Lei	abbia lavorato	sia arrivato/a
noi	abbiamo lavorato	siamo arrivati/e
voi	abbiate lavorato	siate arrivati/e
loro	abbiano lavorato	siano arrivati/e

42.4 Pluperfect subjunctive

The pluperfect subjunctive is formed with the imperfect subjunctive of **avere** or **essere** and the past participle:

	with **avere**	with **essere**
io	avessi lavorato	fossi arrivato/a
tu	avessi lavorato	fossi arrivato/a
lui/lei/Lei	avesse lavorato	fosse arrivato/a
noi	avessimo lavorato	fossimo arrivati/e
voi	aveste lavorato	foste arrivati/e
loro	avessero lavorato	fossero arrivati/e

42.5 Use of the subjunctive

Using the subjunctive generally indicates that the speaker's opinions or feelings are involved.

■ **42.5.1** It is used, introduced by **che**, after a verb expressing:

- possibility or probability:
  È possibile che venga Giorgio.   *Giorgio might come.*

  Può darsi che abbia dimenticato.   *It may be that he's forgotten.*

- opinion:

Suppongo che lei conosca la zona.	I suppose she knows the area.
È strano che lui non abbia risposto.	It's odd that he hasn't replied.

- hope, doubt, wishing or fear:

Spero che torni fra poco.	I hope he comes back soon.
Ho paura che non arrivino.	I'm afraid they won't arrive.

■ **42.5.2** It is used after a superlative:

È la ragazza più gentile che io conosca.	She is the kindest girl I know.
Questo è il migliore vino che abbia mai bevuto.	This is the best wine I have ever drunk.

■ **42.5.3** It is used in expressions like the following:

Fosse vero!	If only it were true!
Dio vi benedica.	(May) God bless you.

■ **42.5.4** It is needed after certain conjunctions, including: **benché** *(although)*, **perché/affinché** *(in order to)*, **purché** *(provided that)*, **a meno che non** *(unless)*.

Te lo dico perché lo sappia.	I'm telling you so that you know.
Lo farò, benché sia inutile.	I'll do it, although it's useless.
Andremo, a meno che non piova.	We'll go unless it rains.

42.6 Subject pronouns

As there is only one form for all three singular persons of the present and the perfect subjunctive, subject pronouns are often used to avoid ambiguity.

È necessario che lo veda **io**.	It is necessary for me to see him.
Non credo che **lei** abbia capito.	I don't think she understood.

42.7 Selecting the correct tense

■ **42.7.1** When the verb before **che** is in the present tense, the present or the perfect subjunctive can be used:

Dubito che vogliano andare. *I doubt they want to go.*

Peccato che non sia venuto. *It's a pity you didn't come.*

■ **42.7.2** When the verb before **che** is in a past tense or the conditional, the imperfect or the pluperfect subjunctive can be used:

Voleva che andassi io.	*He wanted me to go.*
Vorrei che tu fossi qui.	*I wish you were here.*
Pensavo che avesse capito.	*I thought you had understood.*

■ **42.7.3** The imperfect subjunctive is used after 'if' when there is another verb in the conditional (see 32.1.1):

Se vincessi la lotteria, farei	*If I won the lottery, I'd go*
il giro del mondo.	*round the world.*

Similarly, the pluperfect subjunctive is used after 'if' when the other verb is in the past conditional (see 36.3.1):

Se avessi avuto tempo ieri,	*If I'd had time yesterday,*
sarei andato a Firenze.	*I would have gone to Florence.*

42.8 Irregular subjunctives

■ **42.8.1** The following verbs do not form the present subjunctive as in 42.1. For the full tables, see 48.

avere abbia	**dare** dia	**essere** sia
sapere sappia	**stare** stia	

■ **42.8.2** These are irregular in the imperfect subjunctive:
essere fossi, fossi, fosse, fossimo, foste, fossero

bere, dire, fare and verbs ending in **-arre, -orre, -urre** add regular **-ere** endings to irregular stems as in 33.3.2:

bere bev– bevessi **porre** pon– ponessi

43 Reflexive verbs

Reflexive verbs are verbs like **chiamarsi** (*to be called*), **sposarsi** (*to get married*), **divertirsi** (*to enjoy oneself*), which reflect their action back to the subject. They always require the reflexive pronouns **mi, ti, si, ci, vi, si** (see 21).

43.1 Simple tenses

The reflexive pronoun goes before the verb, which in simple tenses is formed in exactly the same way as non-reflexive -**are**, -**ere** and -**ire** verbs.

infinitive	**alzarsi** *to get up*	
present	io	**mi** alzo
	tu	**ti** alzi
	lui/lei/Lei	**si** alza
	noi	**ci** alziamo
	voi	**vi** alzate
	loro	**si** alzano
future	**mi** alzerò	*I'll get up*
conditional	**mi** alzerei	*I would get up*
imperfect	**mi** alzavo	*I used to get up*
simple past	**mi** alzai	*I got up*

43.2 Compound tenses

The compound tenses are formed with **essere**.

perfect	io	**mi** sono alzato/a
	tu	**ti** sei alzato/a
	lui/lei/Lei	**si** è alzato/a
	noi	**ci** siamo alzati/e
	voi	**vi** siete alzati/e
	loro	**si** sono alzati/e

pluperfect	mi ero alzato/a	*I had got up*
future perfect	mi sarò alzato/a	*I will have got up*
past conditional	mi sarei alzato/a	*I would have got up*

■ **43.2.1** Agreement

In compound tenses, the past participle normally agrees with the subject:

Mi sono divertit**o**.	*I (male) enjoyed myself.*
Si è vestit**a**.	*She got dressed.*

... even when there is a direct object:

Mi sono lavat**o** i capelli.	*I've (male) washed my hair.*
Si è cambiat**a** le scarpe.	*She changed her shoes.*

... but when the object is **lo**, **la**, **li** or **le**, the past participle agrees with that instead:

Me **li** sono lavat**i**.	*I've washed it. (my hair)*
Se **le** è cambiat**e**.	*She changed them. (her shoes)*

■ **43.2.2** **Mi, ti, si, ci, vi, si** change to **me, te, se, ce, ve, se** before other pronouns (see 21.3).

43.3 Imperatives

To form the imperative, reflexive verbs follow the rules for non-reflexive verbs (see 41). The reflexive pronoun goes:

... BEFORE the **Lei** imperative:

Lei si alzi	non si alzi

... and AT THE END OF the **tu, noi** and **voi** imperatives:

tu alzati	non alzarti
noi alziamoci	non alziamoci
voi alzatevi	non alzatevi

Non si preoccupi, signora.	*Don't worry, madam.*
Lavati le mani.	*Wash your hands.*
Informiamoci subito.	*Let's find out immediately.*
Accomodatevi.	*Make yourselves comfortable.*

43.4 Infinitives of reflexive verbs

Reflexive pronouns go at the end of an infinitive and combine with it without its final **e**. The forms listed in a dictionary end in **-arsi**, **-ersi**, and **-irsi**:

scusarsi	*to apologize*
sedersi	*to sit down*
divertirsi	*to enjoy oneself*

However, in most cases, the infinitive ending changes and the appropriate reflexive pronoun is used instead of **-si**:

Hai dimenticato di scusar**ti**.	*You've forgotten to apologize.*
Abbiamo voglia di seder**ci**.	*We feel like sitting down.*
Comincio a divertir**mi**.	*I'm beginning to enjoy myself.*

43.5 Reflexive verbs after modal verbs

When reflexive verbs are used after **dovere**, **potere** or **volere**, there are two possible positions for the reflexive pronoun. It can go:

- after the infinitive, which drops the final **e** and combines with the pronoun to form one word:

Devo allenar**mi**.	*I have to train.*
Potresti vestir**ti**.	*You could get dressed.*
Volete riposar**vi**?	*Do you want to rest?*

- or before **dovere**, **potere**, **volere**:

Mi devo allenare.	*I have to train.*
Ti potresti vestire.	*You could get dressed.*
Vi volete riposare?	*Do you want to rest?*

■ **43.5.1** In the perfect tense, reflexive verbs following modal verbs can take **avere** or **essere**:

- with **avere**
  - the reflexive pronoun goes after the infinitive and combines with it
  - the past participle does not have to agree.

  Ho dovuto alzarmi presto. *I had to get up early.*

  Paola, non hai potuto fermarti? *Paola, weren't you able to stop?*

  Hanno voluto dimettersi. *They wanted to resign.*

- with **essere**
  - the reflexive pronoun comes before **dovere**, **potere** and **volere**
  - the past participle agrees with the subject.

  Mi sono dovuto alzare presto. *I had to get up early.*

  Paola, non ti sei potuta fermare? *Paola, weren't you able to stop?*

  Si sono voluti dimettere. *They wanted to resign.*

43.6 Reflexive verbs with parts of the body

When parts of the body or personal items are the object of a reflexive verb, they do not need a possessive adjective. The definite article is used instead:

Mi lavo **le** mani.	*I'm washing my hands.*
Ti sei lavata **i** capelli, Gina?	*Have you washed your hair, Gina?*
Si è tolto **la** giacca.	*He has taken his jacket off.*

44 Modal verbs

The main modal verbs are **dovere** (*to have to*),
potere (*to be able to*) and **volere** (*to want*). They are
generally followed by other verbs. They are written out in
full in section 48.

44.1 Modal verbs + infinitive

Verbs following a modal verb are always in the infinitive:

Deve **cambiare** a Bologna. *You have to change in Bologna*
Posso **fare** il biglietto qui? *Can I get my ticket here?*
Vogliono **prenotare** i posti. *They want to book seats.*

44.2 Modal verbs in compound tenses

In compound tenses, the modal verbs can take **avere** or
essere. They take whichever the infinitive following the
modal normally takes.

Ho dovuto lavorare. *I had to work.*
Sono dovuto partire presto. *I had to leave early.*
Non ha potuto capire. *He wasn't able to understand.*
Non è potuta tornare. *She couldn't go back.*

... but in everyday spoken Italian **avere** is often used
instead of **essere**:

Ho dovuto partire presto. *I had to leave early.*
Non ha potuto tornare. *She couldn't go back.*

44.3 Pronouns with modal verbs

There are two possible positions for pronouns with modal
verbs. They can go before **dovere**, **potere**, **volere** or after
the infinitive, which drops the final -e and combines with
the pronoun(s) to form one word:

Gli vorrei parlare.
Vorrei parlar**gli**. } *I wish to talk to him.*

Me lo può mostrare?
Può mostrar**melo**? } *Can you show it to me?*

44.4 dovere

■ 44.4.1 have to/must/should
In the present tense, **dovere** corresponds to 'have to',
'must' or 'should' ('meant to').

Devo cambiare?	*Do I have to change?*
Dobbiamo partire domani.	*We have to leave tomorrow.*
Dev'essere in ufficio.	*She must be in the office.*
Devono arrivare all'una.	*They should arrive at one.*

■ 44.4.2 had to
The perfect, imperfect, imperfect subjunctive of **dovere** all
express 'had to', but with different shades of meaning:

È dovuto partire	*He had to leave.*
Dovevo andare a scuola a piedi.	*I had to walk to school. (i.e. I used to have to ...)*
Se dovessi scegliere, prenderei questo qua.	*If I had to choose, I would take this one.*

■ 44.4.3 ought to/should
The conditional of **dovere** expresses 'ought to' or 'should':

Dovrei fare uno sforzo.	*I ought to make an effort.*
Dovresti imparare a guidare.	*You should learn to drive.*

■ 44.4.4 should have
The past conditional of **dovere** expresses 'should have':

Avreste dovuto lagnarvi.	*You should have complained.*

The imperfect can also express 'should have', in the sense
of 'was meant to':

Doveva partire ieri.	*He should have left yesterday.*

■ 44.4.5 to owe
Dovere can also mean 'to owe':

Quanto le devo?	*How much do I owe you?*
Mi deve 50 000 lire.	*You owe me 50,000 lire.*

44.5 potere

■ 44.5.1 can/may

In the present tense **potere** corresponds to 'can' or 'may':

Posso aiutare?	*Can I help?*
Può telefonare da qui.	*You can phone from here.*
Possiamo vedere?	*May we see?*

- When 'can' means 'know how to', **sapere** (see 48.15), and not **potere**, is used:

Sa nuotare?	*Can you swim?*
Sanno sciare.	*They can ski.*

■ 44.5.2 could

The imperfect, perfect, conditional and subjunctive of **potere** can all be expressed in English by 'could'.

Potevo aiutare.	*I could help. (I was able/It was possible to help.)*
Ho potuto aiutare.	*I could help. (I managed to help.)*
Potrei aiutare domani.	*I could help tomorrow. (I would be able to help.)*
Se potessi aiutare, aiuterei.	*If I could help, I would. (If I were able to help, I would.)*

■ 44.5.3 could/might

The conditional of **potere** is also used:

- to make polite requests:

Mi potrebbe aiutare?	*Could you help me?*

- to say 'could'/'might' do something, or in the past conditional, 'could/might have' done something:

Potresti almeno aspettare.	*You could at least wait.*
Avrebbe potuto aiutare.	*He could/might have helped.*

44.6 volere

■ 44.6.1 want/will/would

Che cosa vuoi?	*What do you want?*
Voglio uscire.	*I want to go out.*
Vuole firmare qui?	*Will/Would you sign here?*

■ 44.6.2 wanted

The imperfect and the perfect of **volere** can both express the English 'wanted', but there is a difference in meaning:

Volevo uscire.	*I wanted to go out. (This might or might not have happened.)*
Ho voluto uscire.	*I wanted to go out. (And this is what happened.)*

■ 44.6.3 would like/would have liked

The conditional and the past conditional express 'would like to' and 'would have liked to':

Vorrei uscire.	*I would like to go out.*
Avrei voluto uscire.	*I would have liked to go out.*

■ 44.6.4 volere + direct object

Volere is not always followed by another verb. It can also be used with a direct object:

Vuoi un caffè?	*Do you want a coffee?*
Vorrei un cappuccino.	*I'd like a cappuccino.*
Volevo una camera più grande.	*I wanted a bigger room.*

■ 44.6.5 expressions with volere

Volere is used in the expressions **voler bene a** (*to be fond of, to love*), **volerci** (*to take*), **volere dire** (*to mean*):

Vuoi bene a Elena, vero?	*You're fond of Elena, aren't you?*
Ci vuole mezz'ora.	*It takes half an hour.*
Cosa vuoi dire?	*What do you mean?*

45 Impersonal verbs

Impersonal verbs are verbs like **piovere** (*to rain*)
which are normally used in the 3rd person only.
A number of other verbs, such as **bisognare** (*to be
necessary*) can be used as impersonal verbs. The English
translation very often starts with 'it'.

45.1 Verbs which describe the weather

Piove.	*It's raining.*
Nevicava./Stava nevicando.	*It was snowing.*
Tuona e lampeggia.	*There is thunder and lightning.*

45.2 Verbs used as impersonal verbs

accadere/avvenire/succedere *to happen*
bastare *to be enough*, bisognare *to be necessary*
importare *to matter*, mancare *to be missing*
parere/sembrare *to seem*

Non importa.	*It doesn't matter.*
Basta.	*That's enough.*
Succede spesso.	*It happens often.*

45.3 Impersonal verbs + infinitive

Many impersonal verbs can be followed by an infinitive:

Bisogna mangiare bene.	*One has to eat well.*
Occorre allenarsi.	*It's necessary to train.*
Basta firmare.	*All you have to do is sign.*

45.4 Impersonal verbs + che + subjunctive

Some of the verbs in 45.2 can be followed by **che** +
subjunctive, if the second verb has a specified subject.

Pare che sia uscito.	*It seems he's gone out.*
Basta che sia pronto per domani.	*It's fine if it's ready by tomorrow*

45.5 Impersonal expressions

Many impersonal expressions use è + adjective:

è impossibile *it's impossible*, è meglio *it's better*
è necessario *it's necessary*, è probabile *it's probable*
è strano *it's strange*, è utile *it's useful*

They can be followed by an infinitive or by **che** + subjunctive:

È necessario riposarsi.	*It's necessary to rest.*
È necessario che tu ti riposi.	*It's necessary for you to rest.*
È meglio andare.	*It's better to go.*
È meglio che vada io.	*It's better that I should go.*

45.6 Impersonal verbs + direct object

Some impersonal verbs, like **volerci** (*to take*) can be followed by a direct object. When the object is singular, the verb is in the 3rd person singular:

Ci vuole un'ora.	*It takes an hour.*
Basta una bottiglia.	*One bottle is enough.*
Occorre molto tempo.	*A lot of time is needed.*

... but when the object is plural the verb is plural:

Ci vogliono due ore.	*It takes two hours.*
Bastano due bottiglie.	*Two bottles are enough.*
Occorrono molti soldi.	*A lot of money is needed.*

45.7 Compound tenses

Impersonal verbs take **essere** in compound tenses:

È successo l'anno scorso.	*It happened last year.*
Ne sarebbe bastato uno solo.	*One would have been enough.*
È piovuto.	*It rained.*

... but **avere** is often used when talking about the weather:

Ha piovuto.	*It rained.*

46 Verbs followed by a preposition

Many Italian verbs are followed by a preposition when they are used before an infinitive, a noun or pronoun. The most commonly used are listed below.

46.1 Verbs followed by a + infinitive

abituarsi a	to get used to
aiutare a	to help
andare a	to go
annoiarsi a	to be bored
avere ragione a	to be right
avere torto a	to be wrong
cominciare a	to start
condannare a	to condemn
continuare a	to continue
convincere a	to convince
costringere a	to compel
decidersi a	to decide
dedicarsi a	to devote oneself
divertirsi a	to enjoy oneself
esitare a	to hesitate
fermarsi a	to stop
forzare a	to force
imparare a	to learn
impegnarsi a	to undertake
incoraggiare a	to encourage
insegnare a	to teach
invitare a	to invite
mandare a	to send
mettersi a	to begin
obbligare a	to oblige
persuadere a	to persuade
prepararsi a	to get ready
provare a	to try

rinunciare a	*to give up*
riuscire a	*to succeed/to manage*
servire a	*to be used for*
tornare a	*to go back*

Si è fermata a guardare.	*She stopped to look.*
Fra poco mi metterò a studiare.	*Soon I'll get down to studying.*
Sono riuscito ad aprirlo.	*I managed to open it.*
È tornata a leggere il giornale.	*She went back to reading the paper.*

46.2 Verbs followed by a + noun or pronoun

abituarsi a	*to get used to*
assomigliare a	*to look like*
avvicinarsi a	*to approach*
convenire a	*to suit*
dare fastidio a	*to bother*
giocare a	*to play*
insegnare a	*to teach*
parlare a	*to talk to*
pensare a	*to think of*
piacere a	*to please*
rinunciare a	*to give up*
rispondere a	*to reply to*
telefonare a	*to telephone*
ubbidire a	*to obey*
voler bene a	*to be fond of, to love*

Assomiglia molto a suo padre.	*He looks a lot like his father.*
Dà fastidio ai bambini.	*It upsets the children.*
Ho giocato a tennis.	*I played tennis.*
Gli ha insegnato le parole.	*She taught him the words.*

46.3 Verbs followed by di + infinitive

accettare di	*to accept*
accorgersi di	*to realise*
ammettere di	*to admit*
aspettare di	*to wait*
aspettarsi di	*to expect*
avere bisogno di	*to need*
avere fretta di	*to be in a hurry*
avere intenzione di	*to intend*
avere paura di	*to be afraid of*
avere tempo di	*to have time*
avere vergogna di	*to be ashamed of*
avere voglia di	*to feel like*
cercare di	*to try*
cessare di	*to stop*
chiedere di	*to ask*
consigliare di	*to advise*
credere di	*to believe*
decidere di	*to decide*
dimenticare di	*to forget*
domandare di	*to ask*
dubitare di	*to doubt*
evitare di	*to avoid*
fare a meno di	*to do without*
fingere di/fare finta di	*to pretend*
finire di	*to finish*
impedire di	*to prevent*
meritare di	*to deserve*
minacciare di	*to threaten*
pensare di	*to think of*
pentirsi di	*to regret*
permettere di	*to allow*
pregare di	*to beg*
proibire di	*to ban from*

promettere di	*to promise*
proporre di	*to propose*
raccomandare di	*to recommend*
ricordare di	*to remember*
rifiutare di	*to refuse*
sapere di	*to know*
scegliere di	*to choose*
sembrare di	*to seem*
sentirsi di	*to feel like*
sforzarsi di	*to make an effort*
smettere di	*to give up*
sognare di	*to dream about*
sperare di	*to hope*
stancarsi di	*to get tired of*
stufarsi di	*to be fed up with*
temere di	*to be afraid of*
tentare di	*to try*
vantarsi di	*to boast about*
vietare di	*to forbid*

Ho cercato di capire.	*I tried to understand.*
Non mi sento di andare via.	*I don't feel like going away.*
Spero di tornare.	*I hope to come back.*
Ci siamo stufati di aspettare.	*We got fed up of waiting.*

46.4 Verbs followed by di + noun or pronoun

accorgersi di	*to notice*
avere bisogno di	*to need*
avere paura di	*to be afraid of*
avere vergogna di	*to be ashamed of*
fidarsi di	*to trust*
innamorarsi di	*to fall in love with*
lagnarsi/lamentarsi di	*to complain about*

meravigliarsi di	to be surprised at
parlare di	to talk about
ricordarsi di	to remember
riempire di	to fill with
ringraziare di	to thank for
trattarsi di	to be about
vivere di	to live on

Non mi fido del padrone.	I don't trust the owner.
Ti ringrazio dei fiori.	Thanks for the flowers.
Si ricorda sempre del mio compleanno.	He always remembers my birthday.

46.5 Verbs followed by a + person and di + infinitive

chiedere a ... di	to ask ... to
consigliare a ... di	to advise ... to
dire a ... di	to tell ... to
domandare a ... di	to ask ... to
ordinare a ... di	to order ... to
permettere a .. di	to allow ... to
proibire a ... di	to ban ... from
promettere a ... di	to promise ... to
proporre a ... di	to propose to ... to
ricordare a ... di	to remind ... to
suggerire a ... di	to suggest to ... to

Ricorda a Marcello di telefonare a sua moglie.	Remind Marcello to phone his wife.
Gli dica di richiamare.	Tell him to ring back.
Consiglierei a sua sorella di aspettare.	I would advise your sister to wait.

46.6 Verbs followed by da, per, con, in

astenersi da	*to abstain from*
avere da	*to have (something) to*
dipendere da	*to depend on*
giudicare da	*to judge by/on*
guardarsi da	*to be careful of*
passare per	*to pass through*
stare per	*to be about to*
congratularsi con	*to congratulate*
parlare con	*to talk to/with*
entrare in	*to enter*

Ho da fare.	*I have a lot to do.*
Dipende dal tempo.	*It depends on the weather.*
Stavamo per uscire.	*We were about to go out.*
È entrata in casa.	*She entered the house.*

46.7 Verbs which need no preposition

The following verbs are followed by a direct object in Italian, with no need for a preposition.

ascoltare	*to listen to*
aspettare	*to wait for*
cercare	*to look for*
chiedere	*to ask for*
domandare	*to ask for*
guardare	*to look at*
sognare	*to dream about*

Ascoltava la musica di Puccini.	*She was listening to music by Puccini.*
Sto cercando le chiavi.	*I'm looking for my keys.*
Aspettiamo il treno per Roma.	*We're waiting for the train to Rome.*
Ho chiesto il conto.	*I've asked for the bill.*

47.1 -are verbs
parlare (*to speak*)

	PRESENT	FUTURE	CONDITIONAL
io	parlo	parlerò	parlerei
tu	parli	parlerai	parleresti
lui/lei/Lei	parla	parlerà	parlerebbe
noi	parliamo	parleremo	parleremmo
voi	parlate	parlerete	parlereste
loro	parlano	parleranno	parlerebbero

	IMPERFECT	SIMPLE PAST	PERFECT
io	parlavo	parlai	ho parlato
tu	parlavi	parlasti	hai parlato
lui/lei/Lei	parlava	parlò	ha parlato
noi	parlavamo	parlammo	abbiamo parlato
voi	parlavate	parlaste	avete parlato
loro	parlavano	parlarono	hanno parlato

	PRESENT SUBJUNCTIVE	IMPERFECT SUBJUNCTIVE
io	parli	parlassi
tu	parli	parlassi
lui/lei/Lei	parli	parlasse
noi	parliamo	parlassimo
voi	parliate	parlaste
loro	parlino	parlassero

PAST PARTICIPLE	parlato
GERUND	parlando
IMPERATIVE	parla, parli, parliamo, parlate

47.2 -ere verbs
vendere (*to sell*)

	PRESENT	FUTURE	CONDITIONAL
io	vendo	venderò	venderei
tu	vendi	venderai	venderesti
lui/lei/Lei	vende	venderà	venderebbe
noi	vendiamo	venderemo	venderemmo
voi	vendete	venderete	vendereste
loro	vendono	venderanno	venderebbero

	IMPERFECT	SIMPLE PAST	PERFECT
io	vendevo	vendei/ vendetti	ho venduto
tu	vendevi	vendesti	hai venduto
lui/lei/Lei	vendeva	vendé/ vendette	ha venduto
noi	vendevamo	vendemmo	abbiamo venduto
voi	vendevate	vendeste	avete venduto
loro	vendevano	venderono/ vendettero	hanno venduto

	PRESENT SUBJUNCTIVE	IMPERFECT SUBJUNCTIVE
io	venda	vendessi
tu	venda	vendessi
lui/lei/Lei	venda	vendesse
noi	vendiamo	vendessimo
voi	vendiate	vendeste
loro	vendano	vendessero

PAST PARTICIPLE	venduto
GERUND	vendendo
IMPERATIVE	vendi, venda, vendiamo, vendete

47.3 -ire verbs without [isc]
dormire (*to sleep*)

	PRESENT	FUTURE	CONDITIONAL
io	dormo	dormirò	dormirei
tu	dormi	dormirai	dormiresti
lui/lei/Lei	dorme	dormirà	dormirebbe
noi	dormiamo	dormiremo	dormiremmo
voi	dormite	dormirete	dormireste
loro	dormono	dormiranno	dormirebbero

	IMPERFECT	SIMPLE PAST	PERFECT
io	dormivo	dormii	ho dormito
tu	dormivi	dormisti	hai dormito
lui/lei/Lei	dormiva	dormì	ha dormito
noi	dormivamo	dormimmo	abbiamo dormito
voi	dormivate	dormiste	avete dormito
loro	dormivano	dormirono	hanno dormito

	PRESENT SUBJUNCTIVE	IMPERFECT SUBJUNCTIVE
io	dorma	dormissi
tu	dorma	dormissi
lui/lei/Lei	dorma	dormisse
noi	dormiamo	dormimmo
voi	dormiate	dormiste
loro	dormano	dormissero

PAST PARTICIPLE	dormito
GERUND	dormendo
IMPERATIVE	dormi, dorma, dormiamo, dormite

47.4 -ire verbs with [isc] capire (*to understand*)

	PRESENT	FUTURE	CONDITIONAL
io	capisco	capirò	capirei
tu	capisci	capirai	capiresti
lui/lei/Lei	capisce	capirà	capirebbe
noi	capiamo	capiremo	capiremmo
voi	capite	capirete	capireste
loro	capiscono	capiranno	capirebbero

	IMPERFECT	SIMPLE PAST	PERFECT
io	capivo	capii	ho capito
tu	capivi	capisti	hai capito
lui/lei/Lei	capiva	capì	ha capito
noi	capivamo	capimmo	abbiamo capito
voi	capivate	capiste	avete capito
loro	capivano	capirono	hanno capito

	PRESENT SUBJUNCTIVE	IMPERFECT SUBJUNCTIVE
io	capisca	capissi
tu	capisca	capissi
lui/lei/Lei	capisca	capisse
noi	capiamo	capimmo
voi	capiate	capiste
loro	capiscano	capissero

PAST PARTICIPLE	capito
GERUND	capendo
IMPERATIVE	capisci, capisca, capiamo, capite

48.1 andare (*to go*)

	PRESENT	FUTURE	CONDITIONAL
io	vado	andrò	andrei
tu	vai	andrai	andresti
lui/lei/Lei	va	andrà	andrebbe
noi	andiamo	andremo	andremmo
voi	andate	andrete	andreste
loro	vanno	andranno	andrebbero

	IMPERFECT	SIMPLE PAST	PERFECT
io	andavo	andai	sono andato/a
tu	andavi	andasti	sei andato/a
lui/lei/Lei	andava	andò	è andato/a
noi	andavamo	andammo	siamo andati/e
voi	andavate	andaste	siete andati/e
loro	andavano	andarono	sono andati/e

	PRESENT SUBJUNCTIVE	IMPERFECT SUBJUNCTIVE
io	vada	andassi
tu	vada	andassi
lui/lei/Lei	vada	andasse
noi	andiamo	andassimo
voi	andiate	andaste
loro	vadano	andassero

PAST PARTICIPLE	andato
GERUND	andando
IMPERATIVE	va'/vai, vada, andiamo, andate

Andare takes **essere** in the compound tenses.

48.2 avere (*to have*)

	PRESENT	FUTURE	CONDITIONAL
io	ho	avrò	avrei
tu	hai	avrai	avresti
lui/lei/Lei	ha	avrà	avrebbe
noi	abbiamo	avremo	avremmo
voi	avete	avrete	avreste
loro	hanno	avranno	avrebbero

	IMPERFECT	SIMPLE PAST	PERFECT
io	avevo	ebbi	ho avuto
tu	avevi	avesti	hai avuto
lui/lei/Lei	aveva	ebbe	ha avuto
noi	avevamo	avemmo	abbiamo avuto
voi	avevate	aveste	avete avuto
loro	avevano	ebbero	hanno avuto

	PRESENT SUBJUNCTIVE	IMPERFECT SUBJUNCTIVE
io	abbia	avessi
tu	abbia	avessi
lui/lei/Lei	abbia	avesse
noi	abbiamo	avessimo
voi	abbiate	aveste
loro	abbiano	avessero

PAST PARTICIPLE	avuto
GERUND	avendo
IMPERATIVE	abbi, abbia, abbiamo, abbiate

48.3 bere (*to drink*)

	PRESENT	FUTURE	CONDITIONAL
io	bevo	berrò	berrei
tu	bevi	berrai	berresti
lui/lei/Lei	beve	berrà	berrebbe
noi	beviamo	berremo	berremmo
voi	bevete	berrete	berreste
loro	bevono	berranno	berrebbero

	IMPERFECT	SIMPLE PAST	PERFECT
io	bevevo	bevvi/bevetti	ho bevuto
tu	bevevi	bevesti	hai bevuto
lui/lei/Lei	beveva	bevve/bevette	ha bevuto
noi	bevevamo	bevemmo	abbiamo bevuto
voi	bevevate	beveste	avete bevuto
loro	bevevano	bevvero/ bevettero	hanno bevuto

	PRESENT SUBJUNCTIVE	IMPERFECT SUBJUNCTIVE
io	beva	bevessi
tu	beva	bevessi
lui/lei/Lei	beva	bevesse
noi	beviamo	bevessimo
voi	beviate	beveste
loro	bevano	bevessero

PAST PARTICIPLE	bevuto
GERUND	bevendo
IMPERATIVE	bevi, beva, beviamo, bevete

48.4 cogliere (*to pick*)

	PRESENT	FUTURE	CONDITIONAL
io	colgo	coglierò	coglierei
tu	cogli	coglierai	coglieresti
lui/lei/Lei	coglie	coglierà	coglierebbe
noi	cogliamo	coglieremo	coglieremmo
voi	cogliete	coglierete	cogliereste
loro	colgono	coglieranno	coglierebbero

	IMPERFECT	SIMPLE PAST	PERFECT
io	coglievo	colsi	ho colto
tu	coglievi	cogliesti	hai colto
lui/lei/Lei	coglieva	colse	ha colto
noi	coglievamo	cogliemmo	abbiamo colto
voi	coglievate	coglieste	avete colto
loro	coglievano	colsero	hanno colto

	PRESENT SUBJUNCTIVE	IMPERFECT SUBJUNCTIVE
io	colga	cogliessi
tu	colga	cogliessi
lui/lei/Lei	colga	cogliesse
noi	cogliamo	cogliessimo
voi	cogliate	coglieste
loro	colgano	cogliessero

PAST PARTICIPLE	colto
GERUND	cogliendo
IMPERATIVE	cogli, colga, cogliamo, cogliete

Verbs which follow the same pattern include **accogliere** (*to welcome*), **raccogliere** (*to gather*), **sciogliere** (*to melt, dissolve*), **togliere** (*to remove*).

48.5 dare (*to give*)

	PRESENT	FUTURE	CONDITIONAL
io	do	darò	darei
tu	dai	darai	daresti
lui/lei/Lei	dà	darà	darebbe
noi	diamo	daremo	daremmo
voi	date	darete	dareste
loro	danno	daranno	darebbero

	IMPERFECT	SIMPLE PAST	PERFECT
io	davo	diedi/detti	ho dato
tu	davi	desti	hai dato
lui/lei/Lei	dava	diede/dette	ha dato
noi	davamo	demmo	abbiamo dato
voi	davate	deste	avete dato
loro	davano	diedero/ dettero	hanno dato

	PRESENT SUBJUNCTIVE	IMPERFECT SUBJUNCTIVE
io	dia	dessi
tu	dia	dessi
lui/lei/Lei	dia	desse
noi	diamo	dessimo
voi	diate	deste
loro	diano	dessero

PAST PARTICIPLE   dato

GERUND   dando

IMPERATIVE   da'/dai, dia, diamo, date

48.6 dire (*to say*)

	PRESENT	FUTURE	CONDITIONAL
io	dico	dirò	direi
tu	dici	dirai	diresti
lui/lei/Lei	dice	dirà	direbbe
noi	diciamo	diremo	diremmo
voi	dite	direte	direste
loro	dicono	diranno	direbbero

	IMPERFECT	SIMPLE PAST	PERFECT
io	dicevo	dissi	ho detto
tu	dicevi	dicesti	hai detto
lui/lei/Lei	diceva	disse	ha detto
noi	dicevamo	dicemmo	abbiamo detto
voi	dicevate	diceste	avete detto
loro	dicevano	dissero	hanno detto

	PRESENT SUBJUNCTIVE	IMPERFECT SUBJUNCTIVE
io	dica	dicessi
tu	dica	dicessi
lui/lei/Lei	dica	dicesse
noi	diciamo	dicessimo
voi	diciate	diceste
loro	dicano	dicessero

PAST PARTICIPLE	detto
GERUND	dicendo
IMPERATIVE	di', dica, diciamo, dite

Verbs which follow the same pattern include **benedire** (*to bless*), **contraddire** (*to contradict*), **disdire** (*to cancel*), **maledire** (*to curse*), **predire** (*to predict*).

48.7 dovere (*to have to*)

	PRESENT	FUTURE	CONDITIONAL
io	devo	dovrò	dovrei
tu	devi	dovrai	dovresti
lui/lei/Lei	deve	dovrà	dovrebbe
noi	dobbiamo	dovremo	dovremmo
voi	dovete	dovrete	dovreste
loro	devono	dovranno	dovrebbero

	IMPERFECT	SIMPLE PAST	PERFECT
io	dovevo	dovei/dovetti	ho dovuto
tu	dovevi	dovesti	hai dovuto
lui/lei/Lei	doveva	dové/dovette	ha dovuto
noi	dovevamo	dovemmo	abbiamo dovuto
voi	dovevate	doveste	avete dovuto
loro	dovevano	doverono/ dovettero	hanno dovuto

	PRESENT SUBJUNCTIVE	IMPERFECT SUBJUNCTIVE
io	deva/debba	dovessi
tu	deva/debba	dovessi
lui/lei/Lei	deva/debba	dovesse
noi	dobbiamo	dovessimo
voi	dobbiate	doveste
loro	devano/ debbano	dovessero

PAST PARTICIPLE	dovuto
GERUND	dovendo

Dovere can take **essere** in the compound tenses if the infinitive following it normally takes **essere** (see 44.2).

48.8 essere (*to be*)

	PRESENT	FUTURE	CONDITIONAL
io	sono	sarò	sarei
tu	sei	sarai	saresti
lui/lei/Lei	è	sarà	sarebbe
noi	siamo	saremo	saremmo
voi	siete	sarete	sareste
loro	sono	saranno	sarebbero

	IMPERFECT	SIMPLE PAST	PERFECT
io	ero	fui	sono stato/a
tu	eri	fosti	sei stato/a
lui/lei/Lei	era	fu	è stato/a
noi	eravamo	fummo	siamo stati/e
voi	eravate	foste	siete stati/e
loro	erano	furono	sono stati/e

	PRESENT SUBJUNCTIVE	IMPERFECT SUBJUNCTIVE
io	sia	fossi
tu	sia	fossi
lui/lei/Lei	sia	fosse
noi	siamo	fossimo
voi	siate	foste
loro	siano	fossero

PAST PARTICIPLE   stato

GERUND   essendo

IMPERATIVE   sii, sia, siamo, siate

Essere takes **essere** in the compound tenses.

48.9 fare (*to do, to make*)

	PRESENT	FUTURE	CONDITIONAL
io	faccio	farò	farei
tu	fai	farai	faresti
lui/lei/Lei	fa	farà	farebbe
noi	facciamo	faremo	faremmo
voi	fate	farete	fareste
loro	fanno	faranno	farebbero

	IMPERFECT	SIMPLE PAST	PERFECT
io	facevo	feci	ho fatto
tu	facevi	facesti	hai fatto
lui/lei/Lei	faceva	fece	ha fatto
noi	facevamo	facemmo	abbiamo fatto
voi	facevate	faceste	avete fatto
loro	facevano	fecero	hanno fatto

	PRESENT SUBJUNCTIVE	IMPERFECT SUBJUNCTIVE
io	faccia	facessi
tu	faccia	facessi
lui/lei/Lei	faccia	facesse
noi	facciamo	facessimo
voi	facciate	faceste
loro	facciano	facessero

PAST PARTICIPLE	fatto
GERUND	facendo
IMPERATIVE	fa'/fai, faccia, facciamo, fate

Verbs which follow the same pattern include **soddisfare** (*to satisfy*), **sopraffare** (*to overcome*), **stupefare** (*to amaze*)

48.10 parere (*to seem*)

	PRESENT	FUTURE	CONDITIONAL
io	paio	parrò	parrei
tu	pari	parrai	parresti
lui/lei/Lei	pare	parrà	parrebbe
noi	paiamo	parremo	parremmo
voi	parete	parrete	parreste
loro	paiono	parranno	parrebbero

	IMPERFECT	SIMPLE PAST	PERFECT
io	parevo	parvi	sono parso/a
tu	parevi	paresti	sei parso/a
lui/lei/Lei	pareva	parve	è parso/a
noi	parevamo	paremmo	siamo parsi/e
voi	parevate	pareste	siete parsi/e
loro	parevano	parvero	sono parsi/e

	PRESENT SUBJUNCTIVE	IMPERFECT SUBJUNCTIVE
io	paia	paressi
tu	paia	paressi
lui/lei/Lei	paia	paresse
noi	paiamo	paressimo
voi	paiate	pareste
loro	paiano	paressero

PAST PARTICIPLE	parso
GERUND	parendo

Parere takes **essere** in the compound tenses.

48.11 porre (*to put, to place*)

	PRESENT	FUTURE	CONDITIONAL
io	pongo	porrò	porrei
tu	poni	porrai	porresti
lui/lei/Lei	pone	porrà	porrebbe
noi	poniamo	porremo	porremmo
voi	ponete	porrete	porreste
loro	pongono	porranno	porrebbero

	IMPERFECT	SIMPLE PAST	PERFECT
io	ponevo	posi	ho posto
tu	ponevi	ponesti	hai posto
lui/lei/Lei	poneva	pose	ha posto
noi	ponevano	ponemmo	abbiamo posto
voi	ponevate	poneste	avete posto
loro	ponevano	posero	hanno posto

	PRESENT SUBJUNCTIVE	IMPERFECT SUBJUNCTIVE
io	ponga	ponessi
tu	ponga	ponessi
lui/lei/Lei	ponga	ponesse
noi	poniamo	ponessimo
voi	poniate	poneste
loro	pongano	ponessero

PAST PARTICIPLE	posto
GERUND	ponendo
IMPERATIVE	poni, ponga, poniamo, ponete

Verbs which follow the same pattern include **comporre** (*to compose*), **disporre** (*to dispose*), **esporre** (*to expose*), **imporre** (*to impose*), **opporre** (*to oppose*), **proporre** (*to propose*), **supporre** (*to suppose*).

48.12 potere (*to be able to*)

	PRESENT	FUTURE	CONDITIONAL
io	posso	potrò	potrei
tu	puoi	potrai	potresti
lui/lei/Lei	può	potrà	potrebbe
noi	possiamo	potremo	potremmo
voi	potete	potrete	potreste
loro	possono	potranno	potrebbero

	IMPERFECT	SIMPLE PAST	PERFECT
io	potevo	potei/potetti	ho potuto
tu	potevi	potesti	hai potuto
lui/lei/Lei	poteva	poté/potette	ha potuto
noi	potevamo	potemmo	abbiamo potuto
voi	potevate	poteste	avete potuto
loro	potevano	poterono/potettero	hanno potuto

	PRESENT SUBJUNCTIVE	IMPERFECT SUBJUNCTIVE
io	possa	potessi
tu	possa	potessi
lui/lei/Lei	possa	potesse
noi	possiamo	potessimo
voi	possiate	poteste
loro	possano	potessero

PAST PARTICIPLE	potuto
GERUND	potendo

Potere can take **essere** in the compound tenses if the infinitive following it normally takes **essere** (see 44.2).

48.13 produrre (*to produce*)

	PRESENT	FUTURE	CONDITIONAL
io	produco	produrrò	produrrei
tu	produci	produrrai	produrresti
lui/lei/Lei	produce	produrrà	produrrebbe
noi	produciamo	produrremo	produrremmo
voi	producete	produrrete	produrreste
loro	producono	produrranno	produrrebbero

	IMPERFECT	SIMPLE PAST	PERFECT
io	producevo	produssi	ho prodotto
tu	producevi	producesti	hai prodotto
lui/lei/Lei	produceva	produsse	ha prodotto
noi	producevamo	producemmo	abbiamo prodotto
voi	producevate	produceste	avete prodotto
loro	producevano	produssero	hanno prodotto

	PRESENT SUBJUNCTIVE	IMPERFECT SUBJUNCTIVE
io	produca	producessi
tu	produca	producessi
lui/lei/Lei	produca	producesse
noi	produciamo	producessimo
voi	produciate	produceste
loro	producano	producessero

PAST PARTICIPLE	prodotto
GERUND	producendo
IMPERATIVE	produci, produca, produciamo, producete

Verbs which follow the same pattern include **condurre** (*to conduct*), **dedurre** (*to deduce*), **introdurre** (*to introduce*), **ridurre** (*to reduce*), **sedurre** (*to seduce*), **tradurre** (*to translate*)

48.14 rimanere (*to stay, to remain*)

	PRESENT	FUTURE	CONDITIONAL
io	rimango	rimarrò	rimarrei
tu	rimani	rimarrai	rimarresti
lui/lei/Lei	rimane	rimarrà	rimarrebbe
noi	rimaniamo	rimarremo	rimarremmo
voi	rimanete	rimarrete	rimarreste
loro	rimangono	rimarranno	rimarrebbero

	IMPERFECT	SIMPLE PAST	PERFECT
io	rimanevo	rimasi	sono rimasto/a
tu	rimanevi	rimanesti	sei rimasto/a
lui/lei/Lei	rimaneva	rimase	è rimasto/a
noi	rimanevamo	rimanemmo	siamo rimasti/e
voi	rimanevate	rimaneste	siete rimasti/e
loro	rimanevano	rimasero	sono rimasti/e

	PRESENT SUBJUNCTIVE	IMPERFECT SUBJUNCTIVE
io	rimanga	rimanessi
tu	rimanga	rimanessi
lui/lei/Lei	rimanga	rimanesse
noi	rimaniamo	rimanessimo
voi	rimaniate	rimaneste
loro	rimangano	rimanessero

PAST PARTICIPLE   rimasto

GERUND   rimanendo

IMPERATIVE   rimani, rimanga, rimaniamo, rimanete

Rimanere takes **essere** in the compound tenses.

48.15 sapere (*to know*)

	PRESENT	FUTURE	CONDITIONAL
io	so	saprò	saprei
tu	sai	saprai	sapresti
lui/lei/Lei	sa	saprà	saprebbe
noi	sappiamo	sapremo	sapremmo
voi	sapete	saprete	sapreste
loro	sanno	sapranno	saprebbero

	IMPERFECT	SIMPLE PAST	PERFECT
io	sapevo	seppi	ho saputo
tu	sapevi	sapesti	hai saputo
lui/lei/Lei	sapeva	seppe	ha saputo
noi	sapevamo	sapemmo	abbiamo saputo
voi	sapevate	sapeste	avete saputo
loro	sapevano	seppero	hanno saputo

	PRESENT SUBJUNCTIVE	IMPERFECT SUBJUNCTIVE
io	sappia	sapessi
tu	sappia	sapessi
lui/lei/Lei	sappia	sapesse
noi	sappiamo	sapessimo
voi	sappiate	sapeste
loro	sappiano	sapessero

PAST PARTICIPLE   saputo

GERUND   sapendo

IMPERATIVE   sappi, sappia, sappiamo, sappiate

48.16 scegliere (*to choose*)

	PRESENT	FUTURE	CONDITIONAL
io	scelgo	sceglierò	sceglierei
tu	scegli	sceglierai	sceglieresti
lui/lei/Lei	sceglie	sceglierà	sceglierebbe
noi	scegliamo	sceglieremo	sceglieremmo
voi	scegliete	sceglierete	scegliereste
loro	scelgono	sceglieranno	sceglierebbero

	IMPERFECT	SIMPLE PAST	PERFECT
io	sceglievo	scelsi	ho scelto
tu	sceglievi	scegliesti	hai scelto
lui/lei/Lei	sceglieva	scelse	ha scelto
noi	sceglievamo	scegliemmo	abbiamo scelto
voi	sceglievate	sceglieste	avete scelto
loro	sceglievano	scelsero	hanno scelto

	PRESENT SUBJUNCTIVE	IMPERFECT SUBJUNCTIVE
io	scelga	scegliessi
tu	scelga	scegliessi
lui/lei/Lei	scelga	scegliesse
noi	scegliamo	scegliessimo
voi	scegliate	sceglieste
loro	scelgano	scegliessero

PAST PARTICIPLE	scelto
GERUND	scegliendo
IMPERATIVE	scegli, scelga, scegliamo, scegliete

48.17 stare (*to stay, to be*)

	PRESENT	FUTURE	CONDITIONAL
io	sto	starò	starei
tu	stai	starai	staresti
lui/lei/Lei	sta	starà	starebbe
noi	stiamo	staremo	staremmo
voi	state	starete	stareste
loro	stanno	staranno	starebbero

	IMPERFECT	SIMPLE PAST	PERFECT
io	stavo	stetti	sono stato/a
tu	stavi	stesti	sei stato/a
lui/lei/Lei	stava	stette	è stato/a
noi	stavamo	stemmo	siamo stati/e
voi	stavate	steste	siete stati/e
loro	stavano	stettero	sono stati/e

	PRESENT SUBJUNCTIVE	IMPERFECT SUBJUNCTIVE
io	stia	stessi
tu	stia	stessi
lui/lei/Lei	stia	stesse
noi	stiamo	stessimo
voi	stiate	steste
loro	stiano	stessero

PAST PARTICIPLE	stato
GERUND	stando
IMPERATIVE	sta'/stai, stia, stiamo, state

Stare takes **essere** in the compound tenses.

48.18 tenere (*to hold*)

	PRESENT	FUTURE	CONDITIONAL
io	tengo	terrò	terrei
tu	tieni	terrai	terresti
lui/lei/Lei	tiene	terrà	terrebbe
noi	teniamo	terremo	terremmo
voi	tenete	terrete	terreste
loro	tengono	terranno	terrebbero

	IMPERFECT	SIMPLE PAST	PERFECT
io	tenevo	tenni	ho tenuto
tu	tenevi	tenesti	hai tenuto
lui/lei/Lei	teneva	tenne	ha tenuto
noi	tenevamo	tenemmo	abbiamo tenuto
voi	tenevate	teneste	avete tenuto
loro	tenevano	tennero	hanno tenuto

	PRESENT SUBJUNCTIVE	IMPERFECT SUBJUNCTIVE
io	tenga	tenessi
tu	tenga	tenessi
lui/lei/Lei	tenga	tenesse
noi	teniamo	tenessimo
voi	teniate	teneste
loro	tengano	tenessero

PAST PARTICIPLE	tenuto
GERUND	tenendo
IMPERATIVE	tieni, tenga, teniamo, tenete

Verbs which follow the same pattern include **appartenere** (*to belong*), **contenere** (*to contain*), **mantenere** (*to maintain*), **ottenere** (*to obtain*), **ritenere** (*to retain*), **sostenere** (*to sustain*), **trattenersi** (*to stay*).

48.19 trarre (*to pull*)

	PRESENT	FUTURE	CONDITIONAL
io	traggo	trarrò	trarrei
tu	trai	trarrai	trarresti
lui/lei/Lei	trae	trarrà	trarrebbe
noi	traiamo	trarremo	trarremmo
voi	traete	trarrete	trarreste
loro	traggono	trarranno	trarrebbero

	IMPERFECT	SIMPLE PAST	PERFECT
io	traevo	trassi	ho tratto
tu	traevi	traesti	hai tratto
lui/lei/Lei	traeva	trasse	ha tratto
noi	traevamo	traemmo	abbiamo tratto
voi	traevate	traeste	avete tratto
loro	traevano	trassero	hanno tratto

	PRESENT SUBJUNCTIVE	IMPERFECT SUBJUNCTIVE
io	tragga	traessi
tu	tragga	traessi
lui/lei/Lei	tragga	traesse
noi	traiamo	traessimo
voi	traiate	traeste
loro	traggano	traessero

PAST PARTICIPLE	tratto
GERUND	traendo
IMPERATIVE	trai, tragga, traiamo, traete

Verbs which follow the same pattern include **attrarre** (*to attract*), **contrarre** (*to contract*), **distrarre** (*to distract*), **estrarre** (*to extract*), **sottrarre** (*to subtract*).

48.20 venire (*to come*)

	PRESENT	FUTURE	CONDITIONAL
io	vengo	verrò	verrei
tu	vieni	verrai	verresti
lui/lei/Lei	viene	verrà	verrebbe
noi	veniamo	verremo	verremmo
voi	venite	verrete	verreste
loro	vengono	verranno	verrebbero

	IMPERFECT	SIMPLE PAST	PERFECT
io	venivo	venni	sono venuto/a
tu	venivi	venisti	sei venuto/a
lui/lei/Lei	veniva	venne	è venuto/a
noi	venivamo	venimmo	siamo venuti/e
voi	venivate	veniste	siete venuti/e
loro	venivano	vennero	sono venuti/e

	PRESENT SUBJUNCTIVE	IMPERFECT SUBJUNCTIVE
io	venga	venissi
tu	venga	venissi
lui/lei/Lei	venga	venisse
noi	veniamo	venissimo
voi	veniate	veniste
loro	vengano	venissero

PAST PARTICIPLE	venuto
GERUND	venendo
IMPERATIVE	vieni, venga, veniamo, venite

Venire takes **essere** in the compound tenses.
Verbs which follow the same pattern include **avvenire** (*to happen*), **divenire** (*to become*), **intervenire** (*to intervene*), **svenire** (*to faint*).

48.21 volere (*to want to*)

	PRESENT	FUTURE	CONDITIONAL
io	voglio	vorrò	vorrei
tu	vuoi	vorrai	vorresti
lui/lei/Lei	vuole	vorrà	vorrebbe
noi	vogliamo	vorremo	vorremmo
voi	volete	vorrete	vorreste
loro	vogliono	vorranno	vorrebbero

	IMPERFECT	SIMPLE PAST	PERFECT
io	volevo	volli	ho voluto
tu	volevi	volesti	hai voluto
lui/lei/Lei	voleva	volle	ha voluto
noi	volevamo	volemmo	abbiamo voluto
voi	volevate	voleste	avete voluto
loro	volevano	vollero	hanno voluto

	PRESENT SUBJUNCTIVE	IMPERFECT SUBJUNCTIVE
io	voglia	volessi
tu	voglia	volessi
lui/lei/Lei	voglia	volesse
noi	vogliamo	volessimo
voi	vogliate	voleste
loro	vogliano	volessero

PAST PARTICIPLE	voluto
GERUND	volendo

Volere can take **essere** in the compound tenses if the infinitive following it normally takes **essere** (see 44.2).

9 Irregular verbs II

The following verbs are only irregular in the tenses set out below. In other tenses, they follow the same patterns as regular -ere verbs (see 47.2) or -ire verbs (see 47.3, 47.4).

49.1 apparire (*to appear*)

	PRESENT	PRESENT SUBJUNCTIVE	SIMPLE PAST
io	appaio	appaia	apparvi
tu	appari	appaia	apparisti
lui/lei/Lei	appare	appaia	apparve
noi	appariamo	appariamo	apparimmo
voi	apparite	appariate	appariste
loro	appaiono	appaiano	apparvero

PAST PARTICIPLE   apparso

Apparire takes **essere** in the compound tenses.
Verbs which follow the same pattern include **scomparire** (*to disappear*), **sparire** (*to disappear*).

49.2 morire (*to die*)

	PRESENT	PRESENT SUBJUNCTIVE
io	muoio	muoia
tu	muori	muoia
lui/lei/Lei	muore	muoia
noi	moriamo	moriamo
voi	morite	moriate
loro	muoiono	muoiano

PAST PARTICIPLE   morto

Morire takes **essere** in the compound tenses.

49.3 muovere (*to move*)

	PRESENT	PRESENT SUBJUNCTIVE	SIMPLE PAST
io	muovo	muova	mossi
tu	muovi	muova	movesti
lui/lei/Lei	muove	muova	mosse
noi	moviamo	moviamo	movemmo
voi	movete	moviate	moveste
loro	muovono	muovano	mossero

PAST PARTICIPLE   mosso

Verbs which follow the same pattern include
commuovere (*to move, to touch*), **promuovere** (*to promote*)

49.4 piacere (*to please*)

	PRESENT	PRESENT SUBJUNCTIVE	SIMPLE PAST
io	piaccio	piaccia	piacqui
tu	piaci	piaccia	piacesti
lui/lei/Lei	piace	piaccia	piacque
noi	piacciamo	piacciamo	piacemmo
voi	piacete	piacciate	piaceste
loro	piacciono	piacciano	piacquero

PAST PARTICIPLE   piaciuto

Verbs which follow the same pattern include **compiacere**
(*to please, to satisfy*), **dispiacere** (*to displease*), **giacere** (*to
lie*), **tacere** (*to be quiet*).

49.5 salire (*to go up*)

	PRESENT	PRESENT SUBJUNCTIVE
io	salgo	salga
tu	sali	salga
lui/lei/Lei	sale	salga
noi	saliamo	saliamo
voi	salite	saliate
loro	salgono	salgano

Salire takes **essere** in the compound tenses, but see 35.5.4.
Similar verbs: **assalire** (*to assail*), **risalire** (*to go up again*).

49.6 sedere (*to sit*)

	PRESENT	PRESENT SUBJUNCTIVE
io	siedo/seggo	sieda/segga
tu	siedi	sieda/segga
lui/lei/Lei	siede	sieda/segga
noi	sediamo	sediamo
voi	sedete	sediate
loro	siedono/seggono	siedano/seggano

Similar verbs: **possedere** (*to possess*), **presiedere** (*to preside*).

49.7 spegnere (*to switch off*)

	PRESENT	PRESENT SUBJUNCTIVE	SIMPLE PAST
io	spengo	spenga	spensi
tu	spegni	spenga	spegnesti
lui/lei/Lei	spegne	spenga	spense
noi	spegniamo	spegniamo	spegnemmo
voi	spegnete	spegniate	spegneste
loro	spengono	spengano	spensero

PAST PARTICIPLE   spento

49.8 udire (*to hear*)

	PRESENT	PRESENT SUBJUNCTIVE	SIMPLE PAST
io	odo	oda	udirò/udrò
tu	odi	oda	udirai/udrai
lui/lei/Lei	ode	oda	udirà/udrà
noi	udiamo	udiamo	udiremo/udremo
voi	udite	udiate	udirete/udrete
loro	odono	odano	udiranno/udranno

49.9 uscire (*to go out*)

	PRESENT	PRESENT SUBJUNCTIVE
io	esco	esca
tu	esci	esca
lui/lei/Lei	esce	esca
noi	usciamo	usciamo
voi	uscite	usciate
loro	escono	escano

Uscire takes **essere** in the compound tenses.
Riuscire (*to succeed, to manage*) follows the same pattern.

49.10 valere (*to be worth*)

	PRESENT	PRESENT SUBJUNCTIVE	SIMPLE PAST
io	valgo	valga	valsi
tu	vali	valga	valesti
lui/lei/Lei	vale	valga	valse
noi	valiamo	valiamo	valemmo
voi	valete	valiate	valeste
loro	valgono	valgano	valsero

PAST PARTICIPLE   valso

Valere takes **essere** in the compound tenses.

This index lists key words in Italian and English as well as grammatical terms. Many references are included under several different headings. For example:

- you can locate information on the Italian for 'he' and 'she' by looking up 'he' and 'she', '**lui**' and '**lei**', 'pronouns' or 'subject pronouns';
- you can find out whether a verb needs '**a**' or '**di**' before another verb by looking up '**a**', '**di**', 'verbs' or 'prepositions';
- you can check the future tense of the verb '**essere**' by looking up '**essere**', which will direct you to the complete table for this verb; or by looking up 'future tense', which will refer you to the section explaining the future tense and giving irregular forms.